CHEATING LESSONS

CHEATING LESSONS

LEARNING FROM
ACADEMIC DISHONESTY

James M. Lang

HARVARD UNIVERSITY PRESS

Cambridge, Massachusetts & London, England

2013

Library of Congress Cataloging-in-Publication Data
Lang, James M.
Cheating lessons : learning from academic dishonesty / James M. Lang.
pages cm
Includes bibliographical references and index.
ISBN 978-0-674-72463-1 (alk. paper)
1. Cheating (Education)—Prevention.   I. Title.
LB3609.L275 2013
371.5'8—dc23   2013008835

For my father

CONTENTS

CHEATING LESSONS

INTRODUCTION

When I first approached the research literature on cheating in higher education, I came to it without any particular idea of what I wanted to say. My personal experiences with cheating were probably a lot like yours: students occasionally cheated in my classes, it baffled and frustrated me, and I was never sure how to react. I hoped to emerge from the research I was doing with a clearer idea of how I could respond to cheating in my own courses, and with an equally clear idea of how to convey whatever I had learned to colleagues in all disciplines at other institutions. So with high hopes I dug into the existing literature—a very substantial body of research, most of it produced by scholars in fields like psychology and behavioral theory who have spent many years, and sometimes whole careers, seeking to understand the mindset and behavior of the cheating student. Much of that literature took the form of reports on cheating surveys designed to answer some basic questions: What kinds of students cheated? How much did they do it? And, perhaps most important, why did they do it? Because the research in this field has obvious implications for anyone who teaches, almost everything I read concluded with prescriptions on how to combat the problem. I saw many of the same basic sets of prescriptions again and again, and they mostly seemed sensible enough to me. You will find some of them echoed or modified in Part III of this book.

But I also found many of these prescriptions frustrating—not because they did not seem like good and viable recommenda-

tions for addressing the problem, but because they were largely
out of the control of an individual faculty member like myself to
implement. I certainly believed it made sense to work to create
an ethical campus community, for example, and to socialize students into a culture of academic integrity—as Donald McCabe
and his colleagues argue, most recently, in *Cheating in College*—
but my individual efforts to do this affect only a small number of
students on campus each year, and success at such an initiative
depends upon the wholehearted collaboration of my administration and colleagues. What about those faculty members who
are not blessed with colleagues and an administration that will
fully support such efforts? Have they no recourse to reduce the
amount of cheating that takes place in their courses?

While I was puzzling over these questions, I also happened to
be doing some research on recent developments in cognitive
theory, and the implications of those developments for teaching
in higher education. I was reading books and articles on brain
and memory functioning, and conducting interviews with cognitive psychologists for a series of essays I was writing for the
Chronicle of Higher Education. And although I remember no
specific moment of epiphany, it slowly began to dawn on me
that these two very distinct fields could speak to one another—
or that they already were speaking to one another, but not yet
very loudly. Once I saw this connection, I realized that if I
looked at the problem of cheating through the lens of cognitive
theory and tried to understand cheating as an inappropriate response to a learning environment that wasn't working for the
student, I could potentially empower individual faculty members to respond more effectively to academic dishonesty by
modifying the learning environments they constructed. With
this connection in mind, the plan of the book began to fall into
place, and eventually—after the usual series of fits and false starts

that accompany any sustained piece of writing—resulted in what you now hold in your hands.

I wrote this book *as a teaching faculty member* and *for teaching faculty members* in all disciplines first, but I also wrote it for the administrators who support the work of their teaching faculty members. Because these readers may have no specific knowledge about the nature and causes of academic dishonesty, I have begun in Part I with an overview of what the research tells us about the number of students who cheat. I then use four case studies to develop my own theory about how specific features of a learning environment can play an important role in determining whether or not students cheat in our courses. In Part II, I provide guidance for faculty members on how to structure their learning environments in order to reduce cheating and increase learning, taking up in turn each of the four factors described in Part I. In each of the chapters of Part II, I rely on a small number of faculty guides whose work I see as exemplary in their respective areas. But there can be no doubt that cheating happens both within our classrooms and on our campus at large, which means that we have to think not only about how to structure our learning environments in ways that will reduce cheating (and increase learning), but also about how we can best foster a campus culture that promotes academic integrity in our students. In Part III I offer my perspective on how to accomplish that objective, returning to the research on cheating in higher education that supports much of Part I.

Readers who are interested in delving more deeply into the questions I address in Parts I and III, which rely on the data of many experts, should begin by reading a trio of comprehensive overviews: *Cheating in College,* by Donald L. McCabe, Kenneth D. Butterfield, and Linda K. Trevino; *Cheating in School,* by Stephen F. Davis, Patrick F. Drinan, and Tricia Bertram Gallant;

and *Academic Dishonesty,* by Bernard E. Whitley Jr. and Patricia Keith-Spiegel. The heart of my small contribution to understanding cheating lies in Part II, in which I do my best to offer practical arguments about how faculty members in all disciplines can structure learning environments that promote academic integrity by increasing student motivation, student learning, and student self-understanding. David Pritchard, a physicist at the Massachusetts Institute of Technology whose work we will encounter in Chapter 7, once commented to a reporter from the *Chronicle of Higher Education* that "dishonesty reveals flaws in the very way science is taught."[1] I would generalize that statement to include much of the teaching we do in higher education, and flip the sentiment to argue that dishonesty can help us learn how to become better teachers. I hope that both academic integrity researchers and teaching faculty members from all disciplines will find a surprising and helpful juxtapositioning of two very disparate fields of research—cheating and human learning—that may help stimulate new research in both areas, and new strategies for teaching, in higher education today.

PART ONE

BUILDING A THEORY OF CHEATING

Tricia Bertram Gallant, one of the lead researchers on cheating in higher education today, offers an excellent and concise overview of academic dishonesty from 1760 to the present day in her book *Academic Integrity in the Twenty-First Century*. In that history you will find an oft-repeated gem of a quotation from an Ivy League administrator in 1928:

> Many young men and women who are scrupulously honorable in other relationships of life seem to have little hesitancy in submitting themes and theses which they have not written, in bringing prepared 'cribs' to examinations, and in conveying information to one another during the course of an examination. There is a not uncommon feeling that a state of war exists between faculty member and students . . . partly explained by the unsympathetic attitude of some professors, and partly by the rather mechanical organization involving grades, warnings, and probation; but, certainly, the principal cause must be found in the failure of undergraduates to appreciate the value to themselves of serious and conscientious intellectual effort and achievement.[1]

If you come to the problem of cheating in higher education expecting to find evidence that we are in the midst of a cheating epidemic, and that the problem is much worse now than it was in the idyllic past, this quotation will give you pause. The statistics I will present in Chapter 1 should give you even greater pause, and I hope will help convince you that cheating and higher education in America have enjoyed a long and robust history together.

But if you look carefully at this quotation, you will also see in the words of this beleaguered administrator an acknowledgment of the extent to which the learning environments on his campus help exacerbate the problem. He points both to the "mechanical organization" of courses and to the "unsympathetic" attitudes of the professors who teach them. One can easily envision the types of courses to which he refers: the sole responsibilities of the students are listening to lectures, taking exams, and bemoaning their grades; faculty members, by contrast, are both dispensers of knowledge and judges who have no sympathy for students who cannot meet the standardized expectations. While the writer apportions blame to the students for their "failure . . . to appreciate the value" of their educational experiences, one could just as easily point the finger back to the institution and argue that it has failed to convince the students of the value of what it has to offer. In either case, a chasm has opened between the faculty and the students in this description, and that chasm stems at least in part from the extent to which students are uninspired to learn, feel challenged instead of helped by their professors, and see their courses as stumbling blocks instead of steps to a better life.

This might strike some readers as an apt description of today's educational environment, in which the war between students and faculty seems to have evolved into new forms. Yesterday's cheat sheets have become today's smart phones, and the majority of our students still don't come to college with a full appreciation of the "value to themselves of serious and conscientious intellectual effort and achievement." So if you find yourself occasionally frustrated at the reluctance of your students to embrace your courses or your discipline for the pure love of learning, as perhaps you did as an undergraduate, you can rest assured that our faculty forebears felt the same way. Fortunately for us, we have the benefit of several decades of research on how and why students cheat, and that research—much like the quotation above—tells us that the learning environments we construct can have an important influence on academic dishonesty on our campuses. In the three chapters of Part I, I delve into the research on cheating in higher education today, as well as cheating in more generalized learning or performance environments, in order to construct my own theory about the five features of our classrooms and campuses that have the greatest influence on how and why students cheat—and that may also have the greatest influence on whether or not our students learn.

1

WHO CHEATS—AND HOW MUCH?

In the spring of 1962, a doctoral student at Columbia University set out to create the first large-scale estimate of cheating rates in America's colleges and universities. William J. Bowers did not have much to work with in the way of precedents for this research; some previous scholars had attempted to understand the psychological makeup of student cheaters, and a few others had attempted institution-specific studies to gauge cheating rates or investigate possible methods for reducing or preventing cheating. The goal of his project, Bowers explains in his introduction, was "to combine into a single research effort three objectives of previous research—identifying sources of cheating, evaluating remedies, and estimating rates."[1] He began his project by sending questionnaires to the deans of students and student body presidents at "all regionally accredited colleges and universities across the country." He used the responses he received from these questionnaires—which were returned by more than a thousand deans and student body presidents—to construct a survey instrument that was then mailed out, in the spring of 1963, to students at ninety-nine colleges and universities in the United States. The sample of schools in the survey is extremely diverse, including everything from Ivy League schools (Yale) and large public universities (Eastern Michigan) to religious institutions (Notre Dame) and small private schools (Reed).

In the end he received more than five thousand responses to the survey, which makes it far and away the first comprehensive effort to assess cheating rates in higher education in the United States. In the manuscript which he eventually published about his survey, Bowers uses the detailed demographic data that he collected from the students in order to estimate cheating rates for the general student population, as well as to analyze a wide range of what some cheating researchers call *dispositional factors*—in other words, individual features of your personality or your life situation that might *dispose* you to cheat. So in his diligent attempt to ferret out potential dispositional factors, Bowers provides statistical comparisons for just about any aspect of a student's life you can imagine, including the cheating rates of those who dated frequently versus those who didn't, those who spent a lot of time drinking and playing cards versus those who engaged in more wholesome activities, and those who were in college primarily to secure a spouse instead of to learn or improve their job prospects.

Bowers used three different means to try to assess the global rates of cheating among all students in his survey, each of which yielded different results. This fact has made the nutshell conclusion of Bowers's work a difficult one to pin down, and explains why contemporary researchers give varying numbers when they refer to the results of his survey. But most frequently you will see academic integrity scholars citing the second of his three questions, which asked students to indicate whether they had engaged in thirteen very specifically defined behaviors that most of us would consider academically dishonest. Some of these behaviors are the worst sorts of cheating activities that we can imagine, such as "Having another student take an exam for you," "Writing a paper for another student," or "Copying answers from a text or other source instead of doing the work independently."[2] Other described behaviors are ones that we would all likely agree are academically dishonest, but less serious than some of the others, such as "Getting questions or answers from someone who has already taken the exam" or "'Padding' a few items on a bibliography."[3] When Bowers gave students these specific descriptions of academically dishonest behavior, 75 percent of them admitted to engaging in at least one of them over the course of their college career.

If all you know about cheating in higher education today comes from the occasional scandal making its way onto the front pages, or from op-ed pieces or blogs on the subject, this number should come as a surprise to you. The most common plotline you will encounter in contemporary stories or essays about cheating is one which suggests that cheating rates are sky-high and rising. Glancing back at the statistical work of William Bowers can help us see very clearly that this picture gets it exactly half wrong: cheating rates may be sky high—depending on your definition of that unscientific term, of course—but they are not rising. Fifty long years ago, back when our forebears were trading in their bobby socks for bell bottoms and worrying over our entrance into a complicated war in a faraway land, 75 percent of students at America's colleges and universities had cheated at least once in their college career.

Not much has changed since then, at least in terms of the global cheating numbers that concern us here. This will be easy enough for me to demonstrate because the lineage of prominent cheating researchers in higher education passes directly from William Bowers to Donald McCabe, who has been producing large-scale surveys in this area since the early 1990s, beginning just a few years after he left his job as vice president of marketing and sales at Johnson and Johnson for a faculty position at Rutgers Business School. McCabe's early publications suggest a researcher still trying to find his way; titles like "The Measurement of Environmental Volatility" and "Making Sense of the Environment: The Role of Perceived Effectiveness," both published in conference proceedings, give no hint of the long and productive research agenda that McCabe would eventually craft. The first entry in that agenda came in 1991, when he published an essay entitled "Context, Values, and Moral Dilemmas: Comparing the Choices of Business and Law School Students" in the *Journal of Business Ethics* in 1991. Something about analyzing the moral dilemmas of college and university students must have lit an intellectual fire in McCabe, who would proceed, over the course of the next two dozen years, to publish almost fifty articles about student cheating, academic integrity, and honor codes in higher education. In the early 1990s he helped co-found the independent organization the Center for Academic Integrity (now the International Center for Academic Integrity, affiliated with Clemson University) and served as its first president.[4] While you can find plenty of published surveys of cheating behaviors in the literature of this particular subdiscipline, you will not find anyone whose name appears so frequently as McCabe's, or whose work stretches into so many corners of the field.

McCabe's incredibly prolific publication record draws from multiple large-scale surveys he has conducted, frequently in collaboration with other researchers, on cheating among college students. Until 2012, McCabe's body of research and data interpretations had appeared in a very wide variety of formats and publications, all of them short form, from statistical reports in specialized academic journals to more general summary accounts for popular academic magazines like *Change* or the *Chronicle of Higher Education*. In 2012, though, McCabe and two of his frequent collaborators published a monograph, *Cheating in College: Why Students Do It and What Educators Can Do About It*, which provides a handy overview of his entire body of work, stretching from his first surveys in the early 1990s —conducted through the good old U.S. mail—to his most current series of web surveys. I will begin my analysis of contemporary cheating rates with a survey that McCabe and one co-author, Linda Klebe Trevino, conducted in the early 1990s which was designed to replicate Bowers's 1963 surveys. From there, I will move forward to the overview statistics that Mc-Cabe provides us in his recent book about his most current survey results; these two sets of studies give us a thirty- and (almost) fifty-year perspective on Bowers's findings and should help us answer the two pressing questions that most faculty have about cheating rates: How much are students cheating today? And are they cheating now substantially more than they did in the past?

In the fall of 1993, McCabe and Trevino mailed surveys to 500 students at each of nine different institutions, all of which had been included in the Bowers study. They cast a much narrower net than Bowers did, however, in selecting the type of institution from which to draw their survey data: all nine of them were "public institutions of higher education ranging in size from just under 5,000 students to over 35,000 students, with a mean undergraduate enrollment of 12,329 students." They describe the institutions in their sample as "moderately selective in their admission criteria." The total number of students responding to the surveys ended up at around 1,800.[5] In response to our second question, about whether global rates of cheating had increased since 1963, McCabe and Trevino provide a succinct statement of their findings in a 1996 essay in *Change* magazine: "The dramatic upsurge in cheating heralded by the media was not found."[6] In a later summary of their findings published in the academic journal *Ethics and Behavior*, McCabe and Trevino (along with a third researcher, Kenneth D. Butterfield) establish a category of "serious cheating" to cover the thirteen or so cheating behaviors addressed in both studies, and cite a summary rate of 75 percent in Bowers's 1963 survey versus an overall rate of 82 percent in the 1993 replication.[7]

You may be thinking to yourself that a 7 percent increase,

while not huge, certainly counts for something. So let's move forward from that 1993 survey, with its small bump in the overall cheating rate, to the more recent conclusions that McCabe and his colleagues have drawn about cheating rates in higher education, as documented in *Cheating in College*. The most recent data set that McCabe covers in this book comes from an extensive series of web surveys conducted from 2002–2010. Although these surveys come from an eight-year period and cover a huge number of students—almost 150,000 from the United States and Canada—from a range of institutions, McCabe and his colleagues consider them as a single dataset. And that dataset speaks quite clearly about the direction in which cheating rates have moved in the period since their 1993 replication. As McCabe and his colleagues explain, "self-reported cheating recorded in the 2002–2010 web surveys is *lower* than in any previous surveys."[8] In the table that McCabe provides to allow readers to see comparative cheating rates in nine different categories, and which concludes with an overall rate of cheating in his most recent surveys, the rates of cheating come only from schools that do not have an honor code (more on this later). When the honor code schools are removed, the Bowers 1963 survey yields an 83 percent rate of overall cheating; the 1993 replication by McCabe and colleagues yields a rate of 87 percent; the cheating rates for 2002–2010 clock in at 65 percent. According to McCabe's research, then, cheating rates rose somewhat into the 1990s, and then have actually been dropping quite substantially over the course of the past decade.

McCabe and his co-authors, however, are wary of accepting these numbers at face value: "Though we would like to believe that this is an accurate assessment of prevalence," they explain, "we have several reasons to be skeptical."[9] Those reasons stem, in part, from the fact that all cheating surveys, from Bowers to the present day, are based on student *self-reports* of their cheating behavior. As the authors of another book, *Cheating in School,* point out, "we really know what students *claim* to be doing, rather than what they are *actually* doing."[10] And this introduces uncertainty in the numbers in a variety of ways. First of all, it depends upon students trusting that their answers will not be revealed to their teachers—or, as McCabe and his colleagues label it, "concerns about the confidentiality of the electronic data."[11] I suspect that students who put anonymous surveys in the mail to some faraway researcher were more willing to trust the confidentiality of their responses than students who are filling out surveys online, and who are well aware of the many ways we have, in the twenty-first century, to track the identities of anyone with an internet connection. So student self-reporting of cheating behaviors may be lower on the current web surveys for that reason.

Second, and perhaps more substantively, cheating self-reports rely upon the students having a clear understanding of what constitutes cheating—*and* an understanding that correlates with the survey administrator's understanding. Susan Blum, like many other researchers in the area of plagiarism, has pointed out the extent to which today's students have difficulty in distinguishing between acceptable and unacceptable citations from the work of others, in part because of the rise of intertextuality in their lives: "student citation norms differ considerably from academic citation norms. Students accept that in everyday conversation, quotation is fun and playful, though certainly not obligatory; they provide citation only when necessary to direct their peers to rare or unfamiliar sources; they regard the cutting and pasting of pastiche as evidence of originality and creativity; they embrace the notion of collaboration in writing; and they question the possibility of originality in ideas."[12] So it may be the case that when students in today's surveys are asked whether they have ever "plagiarized from public material on papers," they are less clear on what that means, and less likely to respond affirmatively even if they have done so. Another group of researchers confirmed this problem by giving a survey to students on their cheating behaviors, then providing the students with clear definitions of cheating and surveying them again on their cheating behaviors. The self-reported rates of cheating rose after the students had received the definitions.[13] Finally, it may also be the case that students view behaviors that we might count as minor incidents of cheating—such as unauthorized collaboration on homework—as not really cheating at all, and that they only consider really blatant acts of dishonesty as "cheating."[14]

I certainly agree with McCabe and his colleagues that we should not simply trust the raw numbers and accept the story they tell about cheating rates dropping over the past fifty years (after a slight rise in the anything-goes 1990s). I also think it would be imprudent to draw any conclusions in the opposite direction and decide that cheating rates are rising. The data certainly do not seem to support that claim, in spite of what you may read in the news media or hear from your grumpy colleague at the copy machine. But I suspect we can all agree on one point: the rates of cheating are much higher than we want them to be. "No matter how one looks at the data," McCabe and his colleagues conclude, "the prevalence of self-reported cheating is high enough for all of us—students, faculty, and administrators—to be seriously concerned. When more than two-thirds of college students are reporting that they have cheated, we need to pay attention."[15] We do, although we should keep in mind one final caveat about these numbers: they document the number of students who have cheated at least one time in their college careers. We should take seriously all instances of cheating, of course, but the numbers of students who are engaged in frequent cheating is much, much lower. In Bowers's survey, 19 percent of respondents had engaged in at least three cheating incidents;[16] McCabe and Trevino's 1995 survey had that number at 38 percent; a different set of researchers reported in another survey from around the same time that 21 percent were three-time offenders.[17] Not as eye-catching as the global numbers, but still, of course, much too high for comfort.

Indeed it might seem strange to you that, as the author of a practical guidebook on addressing cheating, I just spent several pages trying to convince you that the problem is not nearly as bad as the popular or even academic press might lead you to suspect—that students may actually be cheating less than they did in the past, or at least do not seem to be cheating more than they did in the past. At the very least, we have to acknowledge, as Tricia Bertram Gallant does in the wake of her wide-ranging analysis of cheating surveys back into the past century, that "whether the average twenty-first-century student cheats more or is less honorable than the average twentieth-century student cannot be said with certainty."[18] I see this acknowledgment as crucial because I have come to believe that alarmist arguments about the state of cheating in higher education today lead to alarmist responses, some of which require lots of activity to achieve little effect. In order to address this problem successfully, we have to understand it first.

The particular understanding I want to advocate for in what follows involves turning our attention away from the *dispositional factors* that influence cheating—such as the student's gender, or membership in a fraternity or sorority, and so on—and shifting them to the *contextual factors* that influence cheating. Those contextual factors have been studied and analyzed by cheating researchers now for decades, beginning with Bowers and running through the work of McCabe and his colleagues. But, for the most part, researchers have looked at contextual factors through a wide lens, considering the environment of the campus as a whole, or the living situation of students, or the composition of their peer groups. Much less attention has been paid to what I see as the most relevant contextual factor of all: the classroom environment in which students engage in a cheating behavior. Dispositional factors and campus or peer-group contextual factors certainly are essential to understand and address in our efforts to reduce cheating on campus. If we know that first-year students cheat more than seniors, for example, we can make a smarter decision about the target audiences for our academic honesty initiatives and about where best to expend resources for such programs. But more essential to address, in my mind, is the contextual environment of the classroom itself. When we turn our attention there, the question becomes clear: are there classroom structures and practices that tend to induce (or reduce) cheating? The payoff for asking this question is an obvious one: if we can discover that specific features of a learning environment will reduce or induce cheating, then we have put power in the hands of individual faculty members to address this problem. A faculty member can't make a first-year student into a senior or tell the students whom they should be partying with on the weekends, but faculty members can shape their courses in ways that might reduce both the incentive and the opportunity to cheat.

In order to understand what cheating-relevant contextual factors operate in our courses, I want to step briefly away from the specific context of the higher education classroom and consider more broadly what features of a learning (or performing) environment, in any context, seem to nudge human beings toward or away from the decision to cheat. Once we have considered those features in these more general environments, we will then consider how well they translate back into a college or university classroom—and hence understand more clearly just how much power individual faculty members do have to reduce cheating on campus.

2

CASE STUDIES IN
(THE HISTORY OF) CHEATING

To understand what features of a learning or performance environment might induce human beings to cheat, I want to consider four case studies in which cheating was a well-documented phenomenon: two of them from the more distant past, and two of them from our own time. We will begin, as stories and arguments about western education so often begin, with the ancient Greeks. Instead of taking you to Plato's Lyceum, though, or the groves in which Aristotle strolled and cogitated, or any other landmark of Greek education and philosophy, we open with the Olympic Games.

In his book *The Ancient Olympics,* Nigel Spivey, a historian at Cambridge, provides an excellent overview of the original games, which began in the eighth century BC and ran mostly uninterrupted for more than eleven hundred years (although they took a long hiatus before their revival in 1896). Many features of the ancient games, as Spivey describes them, will sound familiar to the modern reader, despite their historical distance from us. The hero-worship we accord to contemporary athletes, for example, would come as no surprise to the original competitors. Just as the Olympic medalist Bruce Jenner appeared on my childhood breakfast cereal box (and now stars on a reality television show), so the famous ancient Olympian Milo of Croton was celebrated in poems, songs, and statues in the ancient world, including mythologized accounts of his battlefield prowess and legendary death. Today's medalists earn lucrative endorsement deals; successful ancient Olympians could expect to receive—in addition to their iconic wreath of olive leaves—expensive jars of olive oil, cash payments, and various perks in their hometown, including tax breaks, premium theatre seats, and even a lifetime supply of free meals.

Unlike twenty-first-century America, however, in which everyone on the team gets a trophy, and all hard-training Olympians are celebrated for their effort, participants and spectators of the ancient games cared only for the winners. There were no bronze or silver medalists, and losers were occasionally mocked by the versifiers of the day for their weakness or cowardice. "Participation in these games," Spivey writes, "was not, emphatically, about taking part; rather athletes came to Olympia driven by an intense desire to win, to be recognized as the best."[1] Moreover, athletes did not compete against the clock or the historical record in running or chariot-racing events; competition was always live, always against other athletes, with the winner of the final heat or contest taking the sole prize. Athletes trained for months and years in the gymnasiums of Athens and other Greek towns, but when the games arrived, all that mattered was their performance in that one key moment.

With all of this pressure on the individual competition, and the accolades and prizes that redounded to the winner, you would be correct to imagine that the Greeks took the rules of the games seriously. A dozen judges, called the *Hellanodikai*, had responsibilities that included "the conduct of various purificatory rites, the refereeing of events, the levying of fines for offences, and the assignment of prizes."[2] In religious ceremonies prior to the games, athletes took an oath in which they pledged they had trained for ten months prior to the games; judges, for their part, took oaths forswearing bribes and promising to adjudicate fairly.

And yet, in spite of the strict scrutiny provided by the judges, athletes still cheated. The first recorded instance of cheating that Spivey describes occurred in the early fourth century, "when a Thessalian boxer called Eupolos was caught offering bribes to his several opponents."[3] Others followed in the footsteps of Eupolos over the years, according to the ancient traveler and author Pausanias, who recorded some famous instances of Olympic cheating in his ten-volume *Description of Greece* in the second century AD. In the days long before injectable steroids, most of the cheating took the form of bribery—and that bribery, in turn, took many forms. Athletes like Eupolos bribed their competitors to throw a match; athletes also paid off judges; and occasionally, because athletes brought honor and recognition to their home cities and states, athletes were bribed to make false residency claims.

Punishments for cheating of any kind were harsh and public. The judges had the option to administer a flogging to the offenders—this was the fate of Lichas of Sparta in 420 BC, who falsely claimed his winning chariot team as Theban (since the Spartans had been banned from that year's games). More commonly, though, the judges administered heavy fines to cheaters. The money collected from those fines was used to commission statues of Zeus; the statues were erected in a public space of the Olympic grounds with inscriptions memorializing the offense and warning others not to follow their example. Archaeologists have unearthed sixteen of these penitentiary statues—and since the statues were not the only form of punishment available to the judges, we can assume that the number of cheating instances was certainly more than those sixteen statues would indicate.

Given the long span of the games, though, the number of recorded instances of cheating—documented either on the statues or in other historical accounts—remains quite small in comparison to our next three cases. But I would argue that the reason that we see cheating of any kind in the ancient games, despite the harsh penalties and the religious contexts in which they were situated, was because the games provided an intense version of one important feature of a cheating-inducing environment: a strong *emphasis on performance.* Cheating becomes a powerful temptation when athletes are celebrated for their performance in a single contest (or a series of such contests), rather than for the dedication and commitment they put into the training process, or their charitable donations off the field, or any other feature of their public personas. When nothing matters but that one shining moment, it should not come as a surprise that some athletes will choose to do whatever it takes to help them succeed in that moment. The stories of cheating at the ancient Olympics (and of cheating in sports through the present day) suggest that the more pressure you load onto any single performance, the more you are inducing human beings to cheat.

But the emphasis on performance in the ancient games gives us only one of what I see as the essential conditions in which we tend to see cheating flourish, which may help explain why it did not prosper there more robustly. To help bring out the second condition, we now hop in our time machine and leap across centuries and land masses to the civil service exams of Imperial China, which began in the seventh century and continued until the end of the nineteenth century, and which were characterized by a much more rampant culture of cheating.

I was first alerted to the long history of these exams by Susan Blum, an anthropologist who offers a brief account of them in her contemporary analysis of plagiarism in higher education today, *My Word! Plagiarism and College Culture.* Beginning in China's Sui Dynasty, Blum explains, in the early seventh century, and continuing until the first years of the twentieth century, candidates for civil service positions in China were required to pass a series of examinations that tested their knowledge of the works of Confucius and his interpreters. The administration of the exams was like a set of Russian nesting dolls, moving from large district exams all around the country to increasingly smaller and more intense exams in provincial centers, major cities, and finally the palace itself.

Initially established as a gambit by the emperors to dilute the power of noble families, the exams theoretically lay open the prospect of lucrative and respected government careers to just about any ambitious young Chinese man (women were not permitted to take the exams). Practically, that didn't always work out, since the intensity and rigor of the exams necessitated family or independent income that would allow exam-takers to devote many years to study and preparation—not to mention taking the exams themselves, which sometimes required weeks or months of travel to the testing sites. Even with that restriction, the number of men who sat for the initial qualifying exams was tremendous. The available spots, however, were few: Blum cites one estimate that the possibility of passing every exam, and achieving the highest status in the civil service system, was "between one and four in a million."[4]

As Ichisada Miyazaki explains in *China's Examination Hell: The Civil Service Examinations of Imperial China,* the exams evolved over the course of their fourteen-hundred-year history, and each level—district, prefectural, provincial, and so on—had its own specific types of questions.[5] For long stretches of the exam's history, though, the questions required an extremely thorough knowledge of the classic works of Confucianism (the Four Books and the Five Classics), the skill to compose poetry modeled after these same works, and the ability to reproduce verbatim, from memory, selections from an imperial document on education. A typical exam might include a series of questions that asked students to remember and then explicate a set of principles of Confucianism, write a poem with a specific rhyme scheme, and then conclude with the memory test.

The stakes riding on these exams were astronomical. As Conrad Schirokauer explains in the introduction to Miyazaki's book, "the examinations played a large part in determining the composition of the elite, by molding as well as selecting the men who operated the political system and dominated the society."[6] Miyazaki cites a diverse set of Chinese narratives and poems that feature characters either celebrating their passing of the exams or lamenting their failure; in many cases that failure led to subsequent lives of misery and disappointment. And while it was possible to re-take the exams, they were typically held only once every two or three years; each failure meant additional years of trying to support oneself while preparing for another go-around. Stories abound in the literature of men who took and failed and re-took the exams many times in their lives, even into their seventies.[7]

The setting and administration of the exams contributed to their pressure-cooked nature. Miyazaki depicts the administration of the provincial exams, for example, as akin to a grueling and intense rite of passage. On midnight of the day before the three-day examination periods, cannon shots initiated the process of admitting students to the examination compound through the Great Gate. Candidates were gathered into groups under official banners, searched by guards at two separate entry stations, and eventually led though a massive grid of small cubicles, where they found and settled into the tiny spaces they would inhabit for the duration of the examination period. Neither candidates nor administrators could leave the compound during the exam period; the gates were sealed tightly and not opened for any reason. If you had the misfortune of dying during the exams, your body was wrapped up and tossed over the compound wall.

And yet, of course, despite all of these measures (and many more) to ensure the honesty of the exams, cheating flourished.

The range of techniques that were used to enhance exam perfor-mance and beat the exams rivals the range of cheating tech-niques I've seen in just about any other context, including higher education today. In fact, one can almost see precursors or parallels to just about every cheating method that plagues us now, including—to take just three examples—essay mills, cheat-sheets, and illicit communications.

Long before the existence of websites like Essay911 or echeat. com, unscrupulous profiteers in Imperial China were selling es-says to desperate students. Since the Chinese exams focused on such a small range of texts for such a long period of time, exam questions naturally were repeated or modified only slightly from one session to the next. As a result, model answers to common questions were compiled and published for students to memo-rize and trot out during the exams. Local officials, Miyazaki writes, "issue[d] frequent prohibitions of the publication of such collections of model answers, but since it was a profitable business with a steady demand, ways of issuing them surrepti-tiously were arranged, and time and time again the prohibitions rapidly became mere empty formalities."[8]

A 2009 story in the UK newspaper *The Telegraph* reported the discovery of two small books that had been used as cheat "sheets" in Imperial China's civil service exams. One of the two books is described as a masterful feat of miniaturization: "The 160 page text is two-and-a-half inches long and under two inches wide and can fit into a matchbox. It contains 140,000 characters drawn from exam texts."[9] Both books came from professional printers, which reflects the extent to which these memory aids were demanded by nervous test-takers. Candidates smuggled in their illicit test aids in just about every way you can imagine: stashed in their underwear, stuffed into their food, or rolled up and deposited in the hollow shafts of their writing utensils.

We might think about illicit communication as a uniquely modern phenomenon facilitated by cell phones—students communicate answers to one another, both in and outside of the classroom, with their latest technological gadgets. Without that technology available to them, Chinese test-takers still found means to communicate. During the qualifying exams, proctors had ten seals that they could stamp on the papers of students who were suspected of cheating; five of those regulations, including talking or dropping one's papers, were intended to prevent students from communicating during the exams.

The list of methods used by dishonest exam takers could continue for many more pages, even though—as in the case of the ancient Olympics—the punishments for any infractions of the examination rules could be incredibly severe. Miyazaki describes one of the most well-known cheating scandals, which took place during the provincial exams of 1858. A complicated scheme, involving bribery and the passing along of special code characters between test-takers and exam officials, unraveled and implicated candidates and officials at multiple levels. Punishments were meted out according to the rank and involvement of those implicated, from the stripping of all academic credentials to banishment from the capital city. But the five highest-ranking officials, including the Chief Examiner at that time, were sentenced to death. Whatever the scandal or the specific punishment, though, cheaters in China's civil service exams—just like cheaters in the ancient Olympics—could be assured of the public disgracing of their names, and a permanent stain on their character and professional record.

Schirokauer describes the battle against cheating on the civil service exams as a "perpetual struggle," and claims that "to the very end the contest of wits [between cheaters and administrators] remained a draw."[10] The fact that cheating continued uninterrupted for such a long time, in spite of the harshest possible punishments we can imagine, says something important about the small role that threats of punishment play in deterring potential cheaters. When the possibility of the death penalty was not enough to deter cheaters in these important exams, we should not much wonder that the threat of failing an assignment or a course or even expulsion from the institution fails to prevent cheating behaviors in higher education today.

Like the Olympic Games, the civil service exams were certainly characterized by an emphasis on performance, our first essential condition for cheating to flourish. In the exams, as in the Olympics, long periods of training led to a single performance or series of performances in an intense burst of effort. In the case of the civil service exams, the requirements to compose a poem in a single sitting, or to reproduce long passages of classic literature from memory, call to mind the pressures of an athletic competition far more than they do the life of study and scholarship. And in both the Olympics and the civil service exams, no pride came from a noble but losing performance; nor was there great joy in the simple act of joining the contest. The fate of those Olympic athletes or civil service candidates depended entirely on their ability to perform successfully in one highly pressurized moment, not on their noble decision to participate or on giving it their best.

But with both the Olympic Games and the civil service exams before us now, we can add the second condition that may contribute to a flourishing cheating culture: *an emphasis on performance* within the context of extremely *high stakes*. An unsuccessful Olympic athlete could return home and begin whatever career might have been open to him before he embarked upon his Olympic training. Such was not the case for aspiring civil servants; fail the exams, and a career and income ceiling was lowered over your head that remained there for the rest of your life. This key difference helps explain why cheating had a much more substantive place in the exams than in the Olympics. The stakes for both success and failure were much higher for exam takers than they were for Olympians. The history of cheating in the civil service exams suggests to us that ratcheting up the stakes on a performance increases the willingness of human beings to cheat.[11] But to fully understand why Chinese exam takers were more likely to cheat than ancient Olympians—despite the fact that punishments in China were potentially more severe than those in Greece—we make another massive leap forward to our third cheating case, this one involving the public school system of Atlanta, Georgia in the opening decade of the twenty-first century.

This story begins on January 8, 2002, when then-President George W. Bush signed into law the No Child Left Behind Act, a comprehensive educational reform bill designed to create state-based standards for America's elementary and secondary schools.[12] To quote the "Statement of Purpose" that opens the over six-hundred-page bill, "The purpose of this [Act] is to ensure that all children have a fair, equal, and significant opportunity to obtain a high-quality education and reach, at a minimum, proficiency on challenging State academic achievement standards and state academic assessments."[13] The relatively benign and abstract language of that statement hides within it the seeds that will blossom in the city of Atlanta, Georgia in the 2008–2009 school year: "challenging . . . achievement standards" and "state academic assessments." In other words, the purpose of the act is to ensure that students perform well on high-stakes exams.

But here an unusual distinction from our first two cases comes into play. In the case of these standardized exams the pressure falls much more lightly on the students than on the teachers and administrators. I have children who have taken our state's "academic assessments" for many years now, and the threat or administration of the exams never seems to weigh too heavily on their minds. They view the exams as one more school chore they have to undertake, although they are certainly aware of how intensely their teachers seem to emphasize the importance of the exams. Since the exams don't affect the report cards they bring home, however, none of my children has ever shown much distress at a low exam score or elation at a high one.

The same cannot be said for the teachers and administrators over whose heads loom these annual state assessments necessitated by No Child Left Behind. Buried within the provisions of the Act, for example, are a series of steps which the government must take in response to a school that has underperformed on the exams and not responded to a set of initial corrective actions. Those steps include the following:

i) Reopening the school as a public charter school.

ii) Replacing all or most of the school staff (which may include the principal) who are relevant to the failure to make adequate yearly progress.

iii) Entering into a contract with an entity, such as a private management company, with a demonstrated record of effectiveness, to operate the public school.[14]

Hence the state has been given power, as the second point indicates, in the case of schools where students are not performing effectively on the state exams, to fire all teachers and the principal. So here we have an unusual case in which the students are engaged in the performances, but the high stakes have been displaced onto the teachers who are preparing their charges for the exams.

This leads us to the public school district of Atlanta in the summer of 2011, when the Georgia governor released a report that described widespread cheating on the 2008–2009 state assessment exams—cheating *by teachers*, not students. The extent of the cheating and some of the specific ways in which the cheating took place were reported with an almost gleeful indignation by news agencies around the country. Of the 178 educators implicated in the scandal, most were teachers and 38 were principals; 82 teachers confessed specifically to modifying the exams of their students by erasing and changing answers after the exams had been completed. One school held "erasure parties," complete with pizza, where teachers worked together to "improve" the performances of their students on the exams. And, as one newspaper account reported, the cheating activities moved beyond simply erasing and changing answers: "teachers admitted to placing lower-performing students next to high achievers so they could cheat more easily, pointing to correct answers while students were taking tests, and reading aloud answers during testing."[15] The scandal reached right to the top of the Atlanta school system, leading to the public disgracing of the superintendent, who was cited for turning a blind eye to the cheating.[16]

This case helps us see the third essential characteristic of a cheating culture. Although both teachers and former teachers participated in the development of the No Child Left Behind policy and in the creation of the various state assessments, the vast majority of working teachers have absolutely no voice in this process. They see No Child Left Behind as an unwelcome imposition on their professional expertise, and feel unfairly compelled to spend much of the year, especially the latter half of it, "teaching to the test." They have no say in the form or content of the questions that students are required to answer, and they do not score the exams. Many surveys have been conducted to assess the attitudes of America's teachers toward the exams, and they have consistently registered strong negative results. To take just one example, researchers at the University of California–Riverside surveyed 740 of California's most highly rated teachers and reported the following teacher opinions: "Sixty-one percent said

[No Child Left Behind] created an overly narrow conception of the meaning of education; 46 percent felt it diminished creativity; and 59 percent said it had unintended consequences, primarily less creativity in the classroom and increased influence of textbook companies to determine the content and pace of instruction."[17] If you don't believe the statistics, you can come to any dinner party at my house, where my wife and all of our friends who teach spend at least half of every evening together complaining about the ways in which the No Child Left Behind Act has diminished their sense of control of their own classrooms, narrowed the focus of their jobs, and stifled pedagogical innovation.

The gap between the No Child Left Behind legislation and the pressure on the teachers brings to the fore the third feature of a learning or competing environment that induces cheating: *extrinsic motivation.* When an environment compels students to complete a difficult task with the promise of an extrinsic reward or the threat of punishment—rather than inspiring them with appeals to the intrinsic joy or beauty or utility of *the task itself*— that environment lends itself to cheating, since the learners or competitors see the task in question as simply an obstacle to get (or avoid) some external consequence. In other words, in an environment characterized by extrinsic motivation, the learners or competitors care about what happens *after* the performance rather than relishing or enjoying the performance itself.

Again we can note briefly that this condition does not apply to the Olympic Games, which may further explain the lower levels of cheating there. No athlete was forced to compete in the Olympic Games, after all, and no one forced any athlete to participate in any one event over any other. Since the athletes selected the events in which they wished to compete, and voluntarily trained for and competed in the games, we can assume that they did so out of some intrinsic motivation. While they certainly may have wanted fame, glory, or good theatre tickets to go along with their Olympic prize, first and foremost they wanted the prize; as Spivey makes clear in his account, they wanted to be the best in their sport.

By marked contrast, in the case of both the Chinese civil service exams and the Atlanta teachers, the motivation was purely an extrinsic one: a strong performance on the exam brings either an extrinsic reward (a job in the civil service) or the removal of an extrinsic threat (the state will not take my job). But neither exam would seem to create strong intrinsic motivation for the student or teacher to succeed *for the sake of the exam itself.* In both cases the test-takers are subjected to an exam created by an external authority that plays the role of a vetting body: if you pass our exam, you get the prize (or you don't get the punishment). The missing element here, one present in the Olympic Games, is intrinsic motivation to master the exam itself. One can imagine, after all, an Olympic athlete winning the final prize in his sport and being satisfied simply to receive the victory wreath and know that he beat all of his competitors; one can hardly imagine a Chinese exam taker passing all of the exams that would earn him a civil service position and then deciding to return to his village and spend the rest of his days as a shopkeeper. The point of taking the exams was to win the prize, not do well on the exam. Likewise the point of helping your students perform well on state assessment exams is to ensure that your job remains secure. Take away the legislative requirement for state assessment exams to make determinations about school funding or job security and those exams would drop from the curricula of America's schools the day before yesterday.

Our final story, which will allow me to complete the list of conditions that I believe can help to create a cheating environment, moves us out of the messy real world and into a psychology laboratory in Northern Ireland in the spring of 2010, when a trio of British researchers conducted a unique and fascinating experiment in cheating. Working with a group of five-to nine-year-old children from Northern Ireland, the researchers videotaped their subjects attempting to complete a complex "rule-following" task. Standing in a small room, the children had to throw a Velcro ball at a target that was six feet away, using their nondominant hand and facing in the opposite direction from the target. Successfully sticking a ball onto the target—almost impossible for anyone, let alone a young child—would win them a small toy or prize.

Before attempting to complete this task, the children were divided into three different groups. The first group made their throws at the target in the presence of a female observer, who sat quietly in a chair and was instructed by the research team to smile and look friendly, but not offer any help or advice. A second group of children attempted the task in an unsupervised condition, with no adult presence in the room. The third group of children was told that an invisible person named Princess Alice would be sitting in the room with them—but no actual human observer occupied the chair for this group. The children in the Princess Alice group were questioned, both before and after the experiment, about whether or not they believed she was really there; some children believed in her presence, and some did not. This allowed the researchers to divide the children into a total of four experimental groups: those in the presence of an actual human; those who either believed in the presence of Princess Alice or were uncertain about her existence; those who expressed skepticism or disbelief in her presence; and those who completed the task without either a human being or Princess Alice sitting in the room.

The researchers were interested in whether or not the presence of Princess Alice—or, perhaps more accurately, the belief in the presence of Princess Alice—would inhibit the children's willingness to cheat on their task. You can imagine easily enough that a five-year-old child, alone in an empty room, might be tempted to step a few feet over the line or turn and face the target if it would help them win the toy they had been promised; would the "presence" of an invisible observer discourage them from doing so? (Don't feel badly for the children who played by the rules and didn't hit the target, by the way; after a set period of time, one of the researchers came into the room, simplified the rules of the game, and allowed the children to throw until they hit the target and won a prize.)

What the researchers found, unsurprisingly, was that the rates of cheating were lower for those who attempted the task in the presence of an actual female, and higher in the groups that had no observer at all or that expressed skepticism about Princess Alice—and that, hence, believed they were alone in the room, without observation or supervision. But the most interesting result was for the group of children who either believed Princess Alice was present or were uncertain about her; in that group, cheating rates were roughly equal to the rates for those who completed the task in the presence of an actual female observer. So from the two Princess Alice groups, only one of eleven children who suspected or believed in her presence engaged in what the authors call a "full cheating response" (walking up and placing a ball directly on the target); by stark contrast, five out of the seven children who expressed a disbelief in her presence were full cheaters (cheeky little buggers!).

As the authors summarize their conclusions in the discussion section of their paper, which was published in a 2011 issue of the *Journal of Experimental Child Psychology,* "children who professed belief in the invisible person resisted cheating equally to children who performed the same task in the presence of an actual watchful adult. In contrast, the majority of skeptical children fully cheated on the task at some point in the experiment."

The broader and more interesting way to describe the result of their experiment appears in the concluding paragraph of their essay: "those who stated that they believed in the supernatural agent adhered more closely to the rules" than those who didn't. In other words, extrapolating their conclusion to the more obvious point that they don't quite make, belief in the presence of a watchful supernatural presence (and Princess Alice here serves as an obvious stand-in for supernatural agents of any kind, such as God) seems to reduce the amount of cheating in which children were willing to engage.[18]

The fourth feature of a task-completion environment that induces cheating, then, quite obviously, is an *absent God*.

No, just kidding. I will leave that question for the philosophers and theologians to debate, and instead will focus on a more specific feature of this laboratory environment. The researchers in this experiment wanted to design a task that would induce the children to cheat. They did this, at least in part, by giving them an impossible task. A five-year-old child attempting to make a weak-handed throw over the shoulder to a target six feet away will quickly realize that he hasn't a snowball's chance in Hades of winning his toy prize. To borrow the social science language that I will introduce in the next chapter, the children in this situation had extremely low *self-efficacy*—at least in this specific context. However self-confident and successful they may have been in other areas of their lives, they did not believe they were capable of hitting that target. As a result, they had only one recourse to succeed at the task: walk up and put the ball on the target. Princess Alice helps us understand, then, that when learners or competitors lack the confidence in their ability to complete a task successfully, or believe that they have been unfairly given a task beyond their skill or talent level, they are much more likely to resort to cheating.

With that final point under our belts, we can now spell out

more fully and clearly the four features of a learning or competing environment that may pressure individuals into cheating:

1. An emphasis on *performance*;
2. *high stakes* riding on the outcome;
3. an *extrinsic* motivation for success;
4. a *low expectation of success.*

We can see how all of these conditions applied to the Princess Alice study, and hence how the researchers in that experiment actually constructed a near-perfect cheating environment. In addition to giving the students an impossible task, they promised them an extrinsic reward for completing it successfully—a toy. And while a toy might not seem like much of a high-stakes reward for you, put yourself in the position of a five-year old-child, and you might have a different perspective. Finally, in this context, just as in the Olympics, the emphasis was on a successful performance—the children were not given their reward for their throwing techniques, the number of attempts they made, or the amount of near-misses they had. A single successful performance—ball on the target—was all that mattered.

The story of Princess Alice and her charges, along with the other stories in this chapter, help clarify that a new approach toward addressing cheating in higher education may be available to us, if we shift our attention away from the cheater and toward the environment in which cheating occurs. Our students, however, are not greasing up and hurling javelins, or throwing balls at Velcro targets in the lab, so we will move now into the more familiar territory of academic research on cheating, and see the extent to which parallel conclusions can be drawn about these four features of a learning environment in the work of contemporary psychologists and behavioral theorists.

3

"FUDGING" LEARNING ENVIRONMENTS

In the spring of 2012, economist and behavioral theorist Dan Ariely published a book entitled *The (Honest) Truth about Dishonesty: How We Lie to Everyone—Especially Ourselves,* a fascinating account of multiple experiments in which he and a series of colleagues tested the willingness of people to cheat in a variety of situations. In order to make these experiments work, Ariely and his colleagues—like the Princess Alice researchers—had to figure out how to create environments that would allow or even induce people to cheat. They did this in manifold and ingenious ways. Typically they designed an initial task that would help the researchers discern a base level of dishonesty that they would find in an average sample of adult human beings (the control condition); then they modified that task in various ways (the experimental conditions) to see whether the modified condition would induce or reduce the amount of cheating that they observed. So, for example, they created simple mathematical tests that people had to complete in order to earn very small sums of money; the amount of money they earned would increase with the number of problems they solved correctly. In the control condition the subjects would simply return their tests and receive the money from one of the researchers; in one of the experimental conditions, by contrast, they might be asked to score their own test, shred their response sheet, and then simply report orally to the researcher how many problems they had answered correctly. In that condition, as you might expect, the number of "correct" problems reported by the test-takers rose substantially.

Ariely draws an important conclusion from all of those experiments: under the right conditions, most people are willing to cheat a little bit. He calls this the "fudge factor," and uses it to explain a wide variety of lab experiments as well as real-world situations in which unethical behavior seemed to spiral out of control—such as the 2008 collapse of financial markets in the wake of lots of unethical moves made by investment bankers, auditors, lawyers, and more.[1] The comprehensive way in which Ariely and his colleagues tested and confirmed the presence of the fudge factor in multiple situations helps buttress my own arguments about the importance of the environment in inducing (or reducing) cheating. In dozens and dozens of different test conditions, Ariely and his colleagues demonstrated an awareness of how to design situations that *induce* cheating. The researchers in the Princess Alice study had demonstrated this same knowledge: they knew very well how to construct a situation that induced children to cheat. Both sets of researchers seemed aware that if you want people to cheat or not cheat on a task, you don't focus on their gender or their membership in a fraternity or any of the other features of their personality or life situation that might dispose them to cheat; instead, *you modify the environment in which they are completing the task.* As Ariely puts it, in reference to the kinds of dishonesty that take place in our everyday lives, the amount of cheating in which human beings are willing to engage "depends on the structure of our daily environment."[2]

Likewise, as I will argue in what follows, the amount of cheating that takes place in an educational situation may very well *depend on the structures of the learning environment.* The design of the course, the daily classroom practices, the nature and administration of assignments and exams, and the students' relationship with the instructor—all of these are subject to modification in the same way as the conditions of a laboratory, and can be modified in order to induce or reduce cheating. Much of the research and advice on cheating available to us these days focuses instead on the learner, and on how we can better police or modify the learner. Demographic research on who cheats, for example, can help give colleges and instructors better information on determining the kinds of classes in which we should more closely observe students for academic integrity violations. In other words, since students in large courses typically cheat more than students in small courses, we should be more vigilant in proctoring exams in large courses. Or academic integrity education programs, which clarify for students the conventions of academic borrowing and lending, can help them learn to hew more closely to the rules of academic integrity. The approach I am advocating here is not meant to supplant or replace those types of strategies, which can be valuable and effective. But focusing on the learning environment will not only provide an important and potentially effective tool to reduce cheating in our classes—it can also create a sense of empowerment in individual faculty members, who might feel uncertain about their ability to cultivate virtues in their students or police more vigilantly for cheating in their courses.

But, you might be thinking, do you really expect me to modify the conditions of my course in some drastic way just to reduce the small amounts of cheating that might be taking place? I don't, actually. But I am hoping to convince you that modifying the conditions of your course to reduce cheating will also increase the amount that your students are learning—and that those two factors together might induce you to modify your learning environments in a small (and, I hope, manageable) number of key ways. Indeed, the most interesting and exciting discovery I made while writing this book was a very simple one: the environments which reduce the incentive and opportunity to cheat are the very ones that, according to the most current information we have about how human beings learn, will lead to greater and deeper learning by your students.

To give just one quick example of this, consider the rewards that were offered to the subjects in both the Princess Alice experiments and in most of Ariely's studies: money or gifts. Providing money or gifts to people who have successfully completed a meaningless task constitutes an extrinsic reward—that is, as we have discussed already, the reward has no intrinsic or deep connection to the task they completed. Extrinsic rewards, as both sets of researchers seemed to be aware, induce cheating. If the person completing a task or challenge takes no pleasure or satisfaction in the task itself—in other words, if they do not happen to love completing math challenges or throwing balls at targets, and if they do not take deep satisfaction from successfully doing so—then they are more likely to resort to dishonest measures in order to get the task out of the way and receive their reward.

So, too, the literature on human learning has long suggested that offering learners extrinsic rewards for their effort leads to poorer learning. We have an extrinsic reward that we hand out at the end of every class we teach: the grade. And students who focus on the grade as their primary motivation for learning in a course, the research suggests, tend to engage in what the literature refers to as "shallow" or "strategic" learning. The student will seek to learn the material in order to perform well on the paper or exam, and to receive a high grade in the course—but once beyond the exam or the course, will quickly forget it. Sometimes referred to as "bulimic" learning, this binge-and-purge approach to schooling is especially characteristic of students who see grades as their primary motivation.[3] Focusing the attention of our students on their grades, and seeking to motivate them either by promising them high grades or punishing them with low ones, thus should have the dual effect of increasing cheating and reducing learning. Quite obviously, with that information in hand, we should seek to construct learning environments in which students do not see grades as their primary motivators. They should be motivated, instead, by their interest and fascination with the subject matter or the challenge of the assessments, or by the perceived utility of the subject matter for their lives or futures, or by some other factor that drives them to learn the material more deeply from their own internal motives. So likewise, with each of the major features of a learning environment that I will consider in this book, we will find that every modification we can make to a learning environment in order to reduce cheating will also lead to greater and deeper learning by our students.

The four case studies I presented in the previous chapter enabled us to focus our gaze on four specific features of a learning environment that can influence a student's decision whether or not to cheat. As I take up each of those four features in the chapters of Part II, I will draw out more explicitly the way in which those factors influence both cheating and learning. Before we get there, though, I want to bolster my case for the relevance of these four features by noting the ways in which they have been identified and analyzed by researchers who study cheating in higher education (and, in some cases, in education at all levels). But our brief tour through the literature on these classroom contextual factors that can influence cheating will also introduce to us a key fifth feature of a learning environment that can induce or reduce cheating, one that will be thoroughly examined in Part III.

Mastery versus Performance Orientation

We theorized from our survey of the ancient Olympics that a strong focus on performance may help induce individuals to cheat. When a student or competitor has just one shot at a performance, as opposed to multiple opportunities to master or demonstrate a skill, it seems logical that he would be more likely to seek any possible advantage to improve his performance on that one occasion (or very small number of occasions).

The social science literature provides robust support for this theory. Eric Anderman and Tamera Murdock, together or in conjunction with other psychologists, have done a number of studies researching the extent to which the performance orientation of the learner influences students to cheat. The *learner's* orientation is actually a dispositional factor—but, as we shall see shortly, that orientation can also characterize the learner's *environment*. To begin with the orientation of the learner, in a 2006 survey of the research literature on the factors that motivate students to cheat, Anderman and Murdock distinguish between two types of learners in the classroom: "Learners who pursue understanding are referred to as mastery, task, or learning-oriented, whereas those whose primary goal is to demonstrate their ability are termed performance, relative-ability, or ego-oriented."[4] For simplification sake, I will refer here to these two opposing attitudes as "mastery" and "performance" orientations. Anderman and Murdock and their colleagues have found repeatedly that students who have performance orientations toward their courses are more likely to cheat than students who have mastery orientations toward those courses. Performance-oriented students focus on their grades, and hence key in on the major exams or assessments for the course as the most important feature of the learning environment. Thus, like our ancient Olympians, they put more pressure on themselves to succeed at these performances than learners who keep their focus on the mastery of the skill or knowledge being taught, and who have less concern for any specific performance on an assignment or exam.

But these performance and mastery orientations, in addition to characterizing the learner in the classroom, can also be considered as characteristics of *the classroom itself.* So college classroom environments that emphasize grades and competition among students are more performance oriented than classrooms that emphasize learning for the sake of mastery. And the same positive relationship between cheating and performance orientation that we see in students carries over to the classroom structure as well: "Academic integrity also appears to decline when . . . instructors emphasize extrinsic or performance goals over mastery goals."[5] In fact, this link seems to stretch across all educational levels. Anderman and another set of colleagues found the same result in a survey of middle school students: "Students who perceived that their schools emphasized performance goals were more likely to report engaging in cheating behaviors";[6] Murdock and another set of her colleagues found it likewise in a study of high school students who read descriptions of different classroom environments and rated them as more or less likely to induce cheating: "Students rated cheating as more justifiable and more likely when the classroom was portrayed as performance versus mastery oriented."[7] Teachers who seem to focus the attention of the students on a small number of high-pressured assessments, either through the structure of the course or through the classroom climate they establish, create a performance-oriented classroom. And from the ancient Greeks through educational experiments in modern-day America, environments which emphasize performance over mastery may induce cheating.

High Stakes

The more pressure you load onto an exam or assessment of any kind, the more you are likely to have students who respond to that pressure with academically dishonest measures. We saw this in our analysis of the civil service exams in China, which represented a golden ticket to a better life for aspiring civil servants. A thriving cheating culture developed around the exams, which were both high-pressured and performance-oriented. Hoi K. Suen and Lan Yu have argued, in their contemporary analysis of the history of the exams, that the high stakes attending to the exams produced a range of unintended and unwanted consequences, "including rote memorization of model performances [instead of deeper learning or understanding], focusing on test-taking skills, cheating, and negative psychological consequences." In the face of high-stakes exams, they argue, strategies like cheating are "rational behaviors."[8] An excellent example of a piece of social science research that supports this theory has us returning to Asia for a comparative study of cheating rates between American and Japanese students.

George Diekhoff, another frequent contributor to the research on cheating, worked with three colleagues to collect both demographic information and self-reports of cheating behaviors from around 400 American students and 300 Japanese students in the fall of 1994. The authors wanted to see whether the commonly cited Japanese cultural attributes of being "highly conforming, extremely hardworking, education oriented, [and] duty oriented" would produce lower levels of cheating than the authors found in the "more individualistic" American students.[9] Based on these descriptions of the two cultures, one would expect to find Americans cheating more than Japanese. If Japanese students have a stronger sense of duty, and a more substantive orientation to their education, I would certainly expect them to cheat less than students who were more individualistic, and hence perhaps less likely to feel beholden to the abstract community norms of academic integrity. Moreover, the authors note in the Methods section of their paper that the Japanese students in their survey were, on average, slightly farther along than the American students in their schooling. Because previous research on dispositional factors related to cheating had suggested that cheating decreases as students move through their college career, Diekhoff and his colleagues were concerned that this difference between the two survey populations might bias the study to reveal even more cheating in their American sample, beyond what the cultural differences between the two groups of students might produce.

What the authors found was not what you might expect. It turned out that Japanese students cheated at much *higher* rates than the American students. When asked whether or not they had ever cheated on one or more exams during their college career, 55 percent of Japanese students reported in the affirmative, as opposed to just 26 percent of American students. To help explain this very wide discrepancy, the authors point out a key difference between the typical American college course and the typical Japanese course:

> In contrast to colleges in the United States, class attendance is not as important in Japan, especially during the freshman and sophomore years when classes are often huge and professors are less likely to monitor attendance. Professors rarely give regular exams and pop quizzes; therefore, final exams are heavily weighted in determining grades. Thus, studying is not a daily habit for many Japanese students, who study only before major exams. Passing these exams is the primary measure of academic success and the pressure to pass a major exam can be enormous.[10]

Sound familiar? Swap out the word "academic" for "life" in the final sentence and we have a description that could just as easily apply to the civil service exams in China. And in both cases, unsurprisingly, we have lots of cheating. The authors point to these high-stakes exams as the primary reason for the high rates of cheating in Japan: "The Japanese student whose academic success is evaluated by his or her performance on a single major exam may well experience more pressure to cheat than does the American student whose grade is based on a series of shorter exams, quizzes, homework assignments, and the like."[11] The higher the stakes that you load onto any specific exam or performance of any kind, the more you are tempting students to engage in any means necessary to succeed.

Extrinsic Motivation

Our Atlanta schoolteachers, like our aspiring Chinese civil servants, needed to pass (or help students pass) exams in order to achieve some external end. In neither case did the exam takers or facilitators see the process of learning the material necessary for the exam as a good in and of itself; the material or skill must be learned in order to take the exam, and success on the exam means a reward unrelated to the learning itself. I suspect that few Chinese civil servants, for example, were required to write poetry in structured verse forms as part of their daily responsibilities. We saw that the Greek Olympians, by contrast, competed for more than just the awards; they sought to become the best athletes in their sport, to achieve a personal mastery of an athletic skill. I argued in the last chapter that this distinction between the ancient Olympians and the other two cases accounts primarily for the much lower rates of cheating in the shadows of Mount Olympus. When a learner (or competitor) is focused on mastering a skill for the sake of learning or knowing that skill (an intrinsic motivation), they are less likely to cheat than a learner who seeks to pass an exam in order to win an award or avoid a punishment (extrinsic motivations). So our historical examples suggest that the learner's focus on extrinsic rewards, as opposed to intrinsic ones, will lead to greater cheating.

I find the best support for this thesis in the 1963 survey data of William Bowers. Two of Bowers's survey questions asked students to rate how much their grades mattered to them and how much their grades mattered to their parents. When he checked their responses against their self-reported cheating rates, he found that students cheated *less* when they considered grades a high priority, but *more* when their parents placed strong pressure on them to get good grades. Bowers summarized his findings about attitudes toward grades, both the students' and the parents', in this way:

> The more importance students give to 'good grades,' the less likely they are to cheat, no matter how important grades are to their parents. But, holding constant their own evaluation of grades, we find that the more importance they think their parents give to 'getting good grades,' the more likely are students to cheat. In short, the student's own commitment to good grades acts as a deterrent to cheating . . . whereas the perception of parents' commitment to good grades acts as a pressure to cheat. To put this still another way, students are less likely to cheat if their *own* expectations of themselves are high and more likely to cheat if their *parents'* expectations of them are high.[12] (emphasis in original)

Pressure for good grades from a parent, obviously, acts as an extrinsic motivation. It might strike you, rightly so, that grades in general serve as an extrinsic motivator—so why would Bowers have found that students who put pressure on themselves to achieve good grades cheat less than others? The obvious explanation for that finding is that, for a high-achieving student, the extrinsic motivation for grades does not necessarily exclude an intrinsic motivation to learn. Strong students may desire both to learn and to achieve good grades as a result of that learning. I suspect that almost everyone reading this book falls into that category; as both an undergraduate and graduate student you loved your discipline and loved to learn, but you also wanted good grades. I have always been the same way. So the desire for good grades on the part of the student, an extrinsic motivator, does not preclude intrinsic motivators as well.

Not so with the desire for good grades from the student's *parents*, by contrast. Students who seek good grades in order to please their parents seek a reward completely unrelated to their learning: words of praise and acceptance, summer privileges, the avoidance of punishment, and all of the many other carrots and sticks that parents like to use in the raising of children. Those rewards have zero relationship to whatever skill or knowledge the student has learned, and hence function as pure extrinsic rewards; Bowers found a clear and strong relationship between cheating and that pressure for extrinsic rewards from students' parents.[13]

Self-Efficacy

Our Irish target-shooters provided a practical demonstration of the extent to which a low expectation of success can induce someone to cheat on a task. If you can't get the ball on the target by following the rules—and you want the toy—then you break the rules. Likewise, researchers have found that students who have a low sense of self-efficacy—a belief in their ability to succeed—in relation to an academic task are more likely to resort to cheating. This should strike you as unsurprising: if students believe that they are not capable of succeeding on an exam, they will be more likely to cheat. Since the students' sense of self-efficacy obviously resides within them instead of within a professor's classroom practice, this one might strike you as more like a dispositional factor than a contextual one, and if you really wanted to argue with me on that point I would probably concede. I am counting it as a contextual factor because we have the ability, through our course design and our teaching practices, to help or harm students in this area. In a variety of both overt and subtle ways, we are regularly communicating to our students the extent to which we believe in their ability to learn successfully in our courses.

Murdock and Anderman help clarify this, in their overview of research on contextual factors that contribute to cheating, by pointing out that students' self-efficacy beliefs really break down into two separate convictions about one's capacity to complete a learning task: "confidence in their ability to execute the skills needed to bring about a desired outcome" and "their assessments of the contingencies between executing those behaviors and the desired outcome."[14] So first, students have to believe that they have the skills or knowledge necessary to succeed on the task. Second, they have to believe that when they sit down to complete that task, they will be able to do so. This distinction becomes clearer if you think about all of the "contingencies" that might impede capable students from succeeding on a specific exam or assignment: they might feel as if they have not been given enough time; they might worry that they will be hampered by anxiety or illness while trying to complete the task; they might feel as if roommates or other students in the course will somehow interfere with their ability to complete the work (as in, for example, a group presentation). Finally and most important, they might feel as if the instructor will not accurately assess their work or has not provided them with the tools necessary to complete it. So students with a low sense of self-efficacy on a specific exam or assignment might feel as if they do not have the skills or knowledge to succeed, but they might also feel as if some factor out of their control will prevent them from using their knowledge or skill to succeed. I expect that at least one or two of the older Irish school children in the Princess Alice experiment were motivated by the second of these two self-efficacy determinants: when they recognized that the odds had been stacked against their success, they (metaphorically) thumbed their noses at the researchers and cheated in response.

One of the main ways in which this second aspect of self-efficacy has been explored has come in the form of asking students whether or not cheating is justified in the face of poor or unfair instruction. Murdock and Anderman point to one study in which both high school and college students read "19 vignettes depicting a student who was portrayed as having cheated for one of 19 reasons . . . Participants then rated the acceptability of each of these motives. Results indicated that unfair treatment by the instructor was ranked as one of the five most acceptable justifications for cheating."[15] A student who perceives that an instructor will assess her work unfairly will lose her sense of the second form of self-efficacy. No matter what I do for this teacher, she may think to herself, he will not give me the grade I deserve. In that case, she might reason, why bother putting in the work on assignments when they will never receive good grades anyway? Cheating becomes a logical response to such a situation. This form of low self-efficacy may also reflect student perceptions of the unfairness or impossibility of the exam or assignment as opposed to the teacher, according to a survey of high school students by Don McCabe and Daniel Katz: "we tend to see more cheating on tests or assignments that students see as unfair."[16] By contrast, as Murdock and Anderman note, "When students have high self-efficacy beliefs and expect to succeed at an academic task, cheating is probably neither a necessary nor useful strategy."[17]

Influence of Peers

In addition to the four contextual factors identified by our case studies and confirmed in the work of contemporary social scientists, we now have to add a fifth, one that has featured prominently in the work of cheating researchers from William Bowers to the present day: the student's perception of his *peers' cheating behaviors* and his *peers' approval or disapproval of cheating*. In short, if a student believes that his fellow students approve of cheating, and are cheating themselves, he is far more likely to cheat. This should hardly come as a surprise to most college professors, given that they are working with human beings in their late teens and early twenties, when peer approval or disapproval has such a huge impact on almost every aspect of their lives. Students at this age seek the approval of their peers, and that seems to matter as much in terms of cheating decisions in the classroom as it does in their social lives or fashion choices.

Both William Bowers and Donald McCabe have documented the influence of peers as consistently ranking at the top of their list of influential factors. Bowers, for example, asked students to rate the extent to which their peer group—which he defined as "close friends and students they go around with"[18]—would disapprove of their cheating. He then measured those responses against their self-reported cheating rates. The table gives a clear sense of the strength of this measure.

So among the group of students who perceived that their peers strongly disapproved of cheating, only 26 percent of them

Index of perceived peer group disapproval	Percent cheating
Very strong	26
Fairly strong	41
Moderate	49
Fairly weak	59
Very weak	71

reported cheating; for those whose peers did not seem to care whether they cheated or not, more than 70 percent of them reported cheating. As Bowers explains after providing this table, "this relationship is as strong as any we have uncovered so far in the search for determinants of academic dishonesty."[19] Bowers follows this table with several others that control for other factors in measuring this determinant, and concludes that it remains at the top of the list of factors which influence whether students cheat in college.

Donald McCabe and Linda Klebe Trevino, in their 1993 replication of Bowers's survey, found a similar result. "The most powerful influential factors" on student cheating, they report, "were peer-related contextual factors."[20] They break down those "peer-related" factors into three categories, each of which had a significant relationship to self-reported cheating rates: "Academic dishonesty was lower when respondents perceived that their peers disapproved of such misconduct [cheating], was higher among fraternity/sorority members, and was higher when students perceived higher levels of cheating among their peers."[21] The influence of fraternity/sorority membership seems to me more like a specific consequence of the other two factors; the members of a fraternity or sorority have a strong and specific peer culture that can influence them in very positive or very negative ways. I'm sure we have all heard stories of fraternity houses that have file cabinets filled with old papers and tests available to members as study aids or sources of plagiarism. The presence of such academic "resources" sends a strong signal to house members about the extent to which their closest peers and housemates approve of academically dishonest behaviors, and have engaged in them themselves.[22] So the most important determinants are whether or not students observe or learn about cheating among their peers, and whether or not they believe their peers approve of cheating. Cheating rates are significantly higher when the answer is positive in both cases.

Two additional studies by McCabe and colleagues provide even firmer support for this conclusion. In a different survey of over 6,000 students at thirty-one institutions conducted during the 1990–1991 academic year, McCabe (again working with Trevino) listed "perception of peers' behavior" as the most important contextual factor to influence student cheating. They theorized in the discussion section of their paper that "academic dishonesty not only is learned from observing the behavior of peers, but that peers' behavior provides a kind of normative support for cheating."[23] They also suggest in the discussion that students who perceive wide levels of cheating on campus may feel they are at a disadvantage by not cheating, which gives them one more reason to cheat themselves. In the 2004–2005 academic year, McCabe collaborated with two researchers in Lebanon on a cross-cultural study of academic dishonesty at seven American institutions and three Lebanese ones. In both sets of institutions, once again, "student academic dishonesty shows a significant positive relationship with the perceived perception of peers' behavior."[24] In the Lebanese institutions, however, the relationship between perceptions of peer behavior and cheating was so strong that "none of the other independent variables [which they measured] make a significant contribution."[25] As they theorize in their discussion, "perhaps when so many others are cheating around you, it's hard to convince yourself that campus policies and penalties [and other measured variables] are very relevant."[26] In terms of its influence on the decision of the Lebanese students to cheat, nothing else came close to rivaling the influence of their peers.

That concludes the list of environmental or contextual factors that meet two essential conditions: they may influence students' decisions on whether or not to cheat in the classroom, and faculty members have either complete or partial ability to control them. In the four chapters of Part II, we will consider ways in which you can address each of the first four factors we have considered, and work to create a (nearly) cheating-free teaching and learning environment in your classroom. The four chapters of Part III will cover the fifth contextual factor by turning to the larger campus environment in which your classes are situated, and consider how, both individually and in collaboration with others, you can work to create a campus culture of academic integrity. In all of those chapters I hope to convince you that the recommended strategies not only will help reduce cheating in your classes and on campus, but will also draw your classroom environment and teaching practices more closely in line with what we know about how human beings learn, and hence have the potential to make you the most effective teacher possible.

PART TWO

THE (NEARLY)
CHEATING-FREE CLASSROOM

For the past dozen years I have been writing a regular series of columns for the *Chronicle of Higher Education*. For the first half of that stretch, I wrote occasional personal essays about my life as an academic on the road to tenure. Once I had achieved that happy milestone, the column shifted in two important ways: it moved from occasional to monthly, and the focus shifted from my personal life to teaching and learning in higher education. Within the first year or two of starting that column, I became acutely aware of the primary challenge of a regular publication deadline: coming up with a new idea each month. In both my series about my life on the tenure track and my first year or two of columns about teaching and learning I tended to draw heavily from my own personal experience, writing about the specific challenges I had experienced, and trying to describe the ways I had either met or failed to surmount them. After a dozen or so columns in my series on teaching and learning, I felt like I had exhausted the number of personal experiences that I could tap. I had to find a new way to approach the series.

At some point I realized that I could best continue the series by identifying individuals who were doing outstanding work in the practice of teaching and learning and shine a light on them. If I chose my subjects well, I could both bring them some well-deserved recognition and guide other interested faculty to new ideas, new resources, new teaching strategies, new research, new conferences or events, and new ways to think about our work as teachers. In order to help me discover the people who deserved that recognition and had something to offer to the rest of us, I dove back into the world of teaching and learning in higher education—in which I have always kept at least a toe or two—with renewed zeal. I began connecting with faculty from around the country through various social media; I attended more conferences in order to allow me to travel and meet faculty at as many different institutions as possible; I began subscribing to several newsletters and journals on teaching and learning in higher education, and accepted an invitation to join the editorial board of one of them. It wasn't too long before I found myself with the opposite problem from the one that had spurred all of this activity: I now could hardly find time or space to write about all of the fascinating work in higher education that I saw happening all around me.

When I had finished the research for the first couple of chapters for this book and saw what the primary contextual factors were for inducing academic dishonesty, it occurred to me that I knew of faculty members whose research or classroom practices could serve as a model for readers of this book in each of those areas.

I am telling you all of this in order to help explain what you will find in Part II. For each of the first four contextual factors identified in Chapter 2, I have selected a small number of faculty members who will serve as our guides in helping us see how to construct and teach a class that reduces the incentive and opportunity for students to cheat by increasing their desire and ability to learn. In each case I approached my faculty guides—all of whom have received multiple awards and recognitions for their teaching—with a description of this project and asked them if they would be willing to provide their expert assistance; they all agreed readily. In all cases they provided me with course materials and answered interview questions I sent them about both their specific teaching practices and their experiences with academic dishonesty. So you will find me quoting material from personal interviews, from profiles I may have written about them in the *Chronicle*, from their course materials, or from their own published work on teaching and learning in higher education.

Finally, I am shifting slightly the order in which I will address each of the contextual factors we have considered. We will begin with the one that seems most important to me—fostering intrinsic motivation in our students, as opposed to relying on extrinsic motivators such as grades. That strikes me as the most foundational of the five factors that can induce or reduce cheating—it also strikes me as the one that will require the hardest thinking from you, and the most work, in considering how to revise your courses. In some cases, working to foster intrinsic motivation in your students might require you to rethink your course entirely, or rebuild it from the ground up. In the final section of the chapter I consider less drastic possibilities, such as assignment types that might help foster intrinsic motivation within any type of course structure. But if you are going to commit to making one change in your teaching as a result of reading this book, focus on intrinsic motivation first. If your students are not motivated, they are not only more likely to cheat—they are also much less likely to be learning.

The contextual factors taken up in the remaining chapters are ones that you can address through more modest (and less time-consuming) modifications to your teaching. Having said that, I should clarify that I would not expect any readers of this book to put it down and immediately revamp their courses in all four of the ways I will recommend in the following chapters. Unless you have rampant cheating in your classes, such a wholesale revision is probably not necessary. Start more modestly by selecting one or two of the recommended changes and implementing them in your courses next semester. If you find that they have increased student learning in your courses and reduced any problems you have been having with academic dishonesty, try another one. I do believe that implementing all four of these recommended teaching practices is both possible and worthwhile, but I also know how much work it takes to revise a course. Better to start small than not to start at all. I hope that the results of even the smallest start will prove effective, and will inspire you to push yourself a little further with each new semester.

4

FOSTERING INTRINSIC MOTIVATION

We all face the challenge of inspiring our students to develop intrinsic motivation to learn what we have to teach them—as opposed to inspiring them to learn it in order to achieve good grades or receive other extrinsic rewards—but I have always suspected that historians face that challenge more intensively than the rest of us. I can make a relatively straightforward case to students about why they need to develop their writing skills, for example, which will follow many of them into their careers; I suspect you can make an equally compelling case to students about the many ways in which some basic scientific literacy will help them assess and evaluate the many conflicting claims that they will encounter in their lives about matters related to their health or the environment or the possibility that we'll all be whipping around the sky in flying cars sometime soon. How to convince eighteen-year-olds to care about the French Revolution, however, or the fall of the Roman Empire seems like a more difficult challenge to me. It may be for this reason that some of the most interesting writing I have seen about learning and motivation in college and university courses has come from historians such as Susan Ambrose, the Vice Provost for Teaching and Learning at Northeastern University and the lead author on *How Learning Works,* an excellent overview of research on learning theory that you will see cited frequently in these pages.[1]

But the most powerful work on motivation that I have encountered in the literature on teaching and learning in higher education—and perhaps the most powerful work I have encountered on teaching and learning in general—also comes from a historian—Ken Bain, whose 2004 book *What the Best College Teachers Do* has become an essential reference and resource book for many college and university faculty members.[2] I had the excellent fortune to serve for three years as the assistant director of the Searle Center for Teaching Excellence at Northwestern University while Ken was the director, from 1997 to 2000, before I took my first tenure-track job. At that time Ken was preparing to write *What the Best College Teachers Do;* he was in the final stages of collecting and analyzing the materials he had gathered over the past fifteen years on the teaching habits, attitudes, and practices of the most outstanding college and university teachers he had encountered in his career. I was able both to review some of those materials myself and to speak with him extensively about what he had learned from those teachers, and I had multiple opportunities to hear him present his findings to other teachers.

Beginning in the mid-1990s, Ken began offering an intensive three-day workshop on Northwestern's Evanston campus designed to help faculty members from around the country reflect upon and engage with the ideas he had gathered from the outstanding teachers in his study. During that workshop, participating faculty had the opportunity not only to hear about the work of those outstanding teachers, but to meet and interact with them, learning directly from the subjects of the study about the particular innovations that they had pioneered in their courses. For close to twenty years now, that workshop has remained a mind-blowing and career-charging event for the seventy or so faculty members who gather from around the country each year to learn from the most outstanding practitioners in our collective fields of teaching and learning. Several years after I left Northwestern, the workshop followed Bain through several career moves; after he become the provost of the University of the

District of Columbia in the spring of 2012, he began holding the conference each summer in the city of West Orange, New Jersey.[3]

In June of 2012, I returned to the conference for the first time after a twelve-year absence. For three days, while the temperatures outside climbed close to a sweltering one hundred degrees, I was able to reacquaint myself both with the ideas and practices that motivated Bain's work, and with the teachers he both wrote about in the book and has continued to identify and study for his most recent book, *What the Best College Students Do*.[4] So in addition to participating in electrifying workshops on theories of learning and motivation led by Bain himself, I listened in awe as Andy Kaufman, a Slavic languages and literature teacher from the University of Virginia, described for us how his students were teaching Russian short stories and poems to the residents of a local juvenile correctional center; I learned about cutting-edge work in medical education by the Vanderbilt neuroscientist Jeanette Norden; and Charlie Cannon, from the Rhode Island School of Design, walked us through the real-world projects in which students are engaged in his architectural design studios. Although each of the speakers or workshop leaders had a particular focus, the connecting thread among them was how deeply they had each thought about fostering intrinsic motivation in their students. For these outstanding teachers, the most important task they set for themselves was determining how to inspire students to care deeply about what they were learning—to put aside the grade and engage with the material in ways that would create deep and substantial learning.

What struck me just as forcefully, however, was the fact that the innovative approaches these faculty members took to their courses allowed them to create assessments that were virtually uncheatable: their students were engaging with real people, problems, and situations in ways which created unique learning experiences that rendered it virtually impossible for one student or group of students to grab prepackaged material off the internet or pull last year's assessments out of a fraternity file cabinet. The workshop provided a healthy confirmation for me that the most effective means to teach our students are also the most effective means to reduce the incentive and opportunity to cheat. In this chapter, I am going to begin with Ken Bain's research about intrinsic motivation, then consider the work of one of the exemplary teachers he has studied, and whose work I first encountered at that summer workshop. That teacher has focused his attention on his course as a whole, structuring it from top to bottom in ways that are inspiring intrinsic motivation in his students. But you may not have the time or inclination to restructure your course in such a wholesale manner, so I want to finish the chapter with a quick introduction to one of my own colleagues, a psychologist who has found ways to ground specific assessments, rather than wholly restructured courses, in the lives and interests of her students. I hope that by covering this range of possible innovations, from the entire course to the individual assessment, you will be inspired to find a way into a course or assessment innovation of your own, one that increases intrinsic motivation—and, in the process, reduces cheating.

Ken Bain's Best Teachers

"People learn best," Bain writes in *What the Best College Teachers Do,* "when they ask an important question that they care about answering, or adopt a goal that they want to reach . . . If we are not seeking an answer to anything, we pay little attention to random information."[5] This should not come as surprising to us if we stop and think about it; we are inspired to learn about topics that we already care about, or that are able to capture our attention when we first encounter them. Bain's research on learning and motivation suggests two possible avenues for teachers seeking to light the intrinsic fires of their students. First, you might engage students in your course by centering the course on questions or issues that you know the students already care deeply about. That doesn't mean pandering to whatever topics happen to be in *Sports Illustrated* or *Glamour* magazine that week. As Bain explains, the subjects of his study accomplish this task "primarily by helping students see the connection between the questions of the course and the questions that students might bring to the course."[6] Students, like all of us, want the answers to questions, both big and small, about their lives and their futures and their world. They are anxious to know what awaits them in the world beyond college; they might be encountering death and infirmity for the first time with aging grandparents; they struggle with money and sex and morality. In all of these areas they have questions, and thinking about how our courses tie into these big questions can help create connections between their concerns and ours.

Bain, for example, mentions an early-twentieth-century historical event that he has covered in his history courses: the formation of the League of Nations after World War I and the decisions that US president Woodrow Wilson made in attempting to convince the US Senate to join the newly formed international organization. As you might imagine, asking students to care about such a seemingly arcane historical matter might prove challenging to any teacher of history. But Bain painstakingly traces the reasons why historians might take an interest in such an event, focusing on the question of whether Wilson might have made different decisions and taken a different course of action. If he had, might he have ultimately prevented World War II? This inquiry leads Bain to the biggest question of all: "Can people control their own destiny, or does some kind of determinism, economic or otherwise, sweep us along, making us hapless observers and chroniclers of our own fate and the antics of even a powerful individual such as Woodrow Wilson insignificant?"[7] That's the kind of question in which any human being should take an interest; the trick for the historian is to help students understand how a close analysis of the Woodrow Wilson story might help us meditate more deeply about it.

A second way to think about Bain's research on motivation and learning, instead of trying to seek out and connect with the specific questions the students already have, is to present to the students intriguing or fascinating or puzzling stories and problems and to encourage them to develop their own questions about those stories or problems. "The people we explored," Bain writes, "know the value that intellectual challenges—even inducing puzzlement and confusion—can play in stimulating interest in the questions of their courses."[8] This approach might make most sense in upper-level courses, where students already have an interest in the discipline and are more likely to find themselves hooked by a terrific story or a curious problem. The key to this approach is to present to the students the problem or challenge and then let them develop their own questions, rather than trotting them through a series of sub-questions that you have already outlined for them. So in the end, like the first approach, this one establishes an environment in which students are driven by *their* questions instead of *yours*. I should note that this approach will only work if you present to the students big, real, and relatively unstructured problems or challenges. Your conundrums will not count as intriguing challenges or fascinating problems if *you* don't still see them as such, and if they do not exist within large and unstructured domains that allow for approaches from multiple angles, or questions from multiple perspectives. I have always noticed that my literature classes become the most interesting and energized when I am teaching a work for the first time and have not yet fully formed my own theories and ideas about the work. In those classes, I am much more open to simply letting the students drive the discussion, rather than trying to lead them by the nose through my pet theories about the text.

I would argue that we need to add one final element to our courses if we want to foster intrinsic motivation, in addition to constructing them in ways that either connect them to students' pre-existing questions or inspire them with fascinating challenges or problems. We have to give the students opportunities to respond in authentic ways over which they have some control. We don't want to pose a fascinating question to our students and then allow them to answer that question only through a multiple-choice exam. To foster intrinsic motivation, we have to think more creatively than that, or at least more flexibly, and give students the choice to respond in ways that emerge from their grappling with those questions.

To consider each of these elements in greater depth, let's turn to the work of Andy Kaufman, and to the University of Virginia students who spend their semester teaching classic works of Russian literature to the residents of a local juvenile correctional center.

Andy Kaufman's Big Challenge

The first time that Andy Kaufman taught in a correctional center, a prison fight broke out while he was being escorted to his classroom. The guard and chaplain who were accompanying him quickly shuffled him into a locked room, where they spent thirty minutes waiting out the melee. After calm had been restored, and he continued his walk down the corridors of the facility, Kaufman could see prisoners standing or sitting in the small cells they passed. He was struck by the size of the rooms, which he guessed were no more than 150 feet square and were crowded with beds and metal sinks and latrines. "I grew claustrophobic just looking into them," Kaufman told me in an interview.[9]

When he finally made it into the classroom at the nearby Virginia correctional center—where he had agreed to teach a class on Russian literature to a small group of inmates as part of a celebration of reading sponsored by the National Endowment for the Arts—nervously clutching his notes for an introductory lecture on *The Death of Ivan Ilyich,* he found himself facing fifteen men in orange jumpsuits and wondered whether they would care about a word he said. Like every good teacher has to do from time to time, he assessed the situation at hand and made a quick decision to abandon his prepared lesson plan and adjust his teaching to the faces in the room.

"So what did reading *The Death of Ivan Ilyich,*" he said to them, "mean to *you?*"

Much to his surprise, Leo Tolstoy's novella of the unexplained and unexpected death of a Russian judge living in the 1880s meant many things to those inmates. After a brief period of uncomfortable silence—the kind to which we are all accustomed, and have to learn to sit through if we want our students to add their voices to our classrooms—the inmates began to speak to Kaufman about what they had learned from Ivan Ilyich. "How you treat people," one of the inmates ventured, "you know, how he treated people as judge—that's how he was gonna get treated as a patient." Another pointed out that while it was too late for Ivan Ilyich to change his life, it was not too late for the inmates. They had to learn to take better advantage of the time they had left.

Ninety minutes later, Kaufman realized that his time in that prison classroom had been a powerful learning experience for him, reigniting his passion for the great works of literature that he had spent countless hours analyzing in more technical ways or writing about in his scholarship. As he explained in an essay he sent me about the experience:

> By moving outside of my comfort zone, by experiencing the work in a radically unfamiliar context, I was able to rediscover its power and relevance for myself. Russian formalists introduced the concept of *ostranenie*—making the familiar appear unfamiliar—as the means by which a work of art gains force to affect thought and emotions. What I experienced on that day was a classic case of *ostranenie*. It felt as if I were encountering Tolstoy's great novella for the very first time.

That the experience could have made Kaufman feel as if he were encountering the work for the first time is all the more striking when you note Kaufman's academic credentials: the author of *Understanding Tolstoy,* published in 2011 by the Ohio State University Press; a lecturer in the Department of Slavic Languages and Literatures at the University of Virginia; and the author of a forthcoming crossover book on Tolstoy's most famous novel, *War and Peace.* But we all know that scholarly and professional accomplishments like these can come to feel, over the course of a career, like extrinsic motivations through which we drift away from our real love for our subject matter. What Kaufman rediscovered in that prison classroom was his own intrinsic motivation for studying the great works of Russian literature. The responses of the inmates helped him remember the power of literature to transform lives. In the room full of prisoners, he says, "I was forced to have authentic conversations with inmates about things that matter to all of us as human beings and not merely things that matter to me as a professional academic." As well as reigniting his passion for his subject matter, those conversations revealed new ways of understanding and analyzing the story. The prisoners brought to the discussion table experiences with isolation and alienation and despair that helped Kaufman rethink elements of the story he had once taken for granted.

Kaufman continued to reflect on his experiences for weeks and months after his visit to the correctional center, wondering how he could provide for his university students the kind of transformative and intrinsically motivating encounter with the literature—and with other human beings—that he had experienced. The eventual result of his reflections was Books Behind Bars: Life, Literature, and Leadership, a course at the University of Virginia in which Kaufman's students study selected shorter classics of Russian literature and then teach them to the residents of a juvenile correctional center near the University of Virginia campus. Kaufman has been teaching the class since the spring of 2010, and it has become a mind- and life-changing experience for Kaufman, for the students who sign up each semester, and for the residents of the correctional center. The students in Kaufman's course undergo a condensed version of his experience as a scholar and teacher of Russian literature. They spend the first weeks of the semester seeking to analyze and understand the themes of the works on the syllabus in formalized and historically contextualized ways, and then spend the middle and final weeks of the semester seeing how those themes become meaningful to the human beings sitting in front of them. In their class meetings on campus the students work in small groups to prepare lesson or discussion plans for the residents of the correctional center; in their meetings at the correctional center, they let the concerns and comments and reactions of the residents drive their discussions. Ultimately, Kaufman explained in a radio broadcast about the course, the students and the residents are holding "conversations about life, through literature, about things that really matter to them."[10] Those conversations are the purpose of the course.

It should come as no surprise, when the course's purpose

is characterized in this way, that Kaufman's students find the course such an amazing and intrinsically motivating learning experience. Note first that Kaufman wants the students to have conversations about things that matter *to them*—i.e., both the residents and the students—instead of about things that matter *to him*. In March of 2011, Kaufman and one of his students from the course wrote companion essays about their experiences for the Inside Higher Ed website. The student, Hannah Ehrlinspiel, notes specifically the disconnect she had been accustomed to experiencing between the study of literature and any real or meaningful connections to her own life: "*real,* personal relevance and human connection had often been discouraged in my other classes." Hence it proved difficult for her at first to hold conversations with the residents in which those connections became central. But once those conversations began to blossom, she was reminded—just as Kaufman was reminded in his prison teaching experience—that "the questions raised by great literature are actually the most important questions raised by life itself."[11] Multiple students in Kaufman's course have been interviewed for a long-term study of the course's impact, and they speak again and again in those interviews on the way in which the course helped them see the relevance of the literature to their lives, the lives of the residents, and the world around them today.

But such relevance was not found by simply skating over the surface of the works and finding easy points of connection. The students were motivated by their encounters with the residents to dig more deeply into the works than they otherwise might have, in order to help ensure that they were well prepared. As Ehrlinspiel explains:

> For years I had always been taught that literature was something
> you had to stab at, to pick through until it gave up its most com-

plex secrets. "Books Behind Bars," however, taught me to appreciate simplicity, to yield to the most basic stirrings of emotion caused by a genuine smile or by a beautiful simile. As a result, I got much closer to the texts than ever before, and became genuinely interested in what each work really *means*.[12]

In college-level courses of literature we don't spend too much time thinking or worrying about the "basic stirrings of emotion" that works of literature inspire in our students. We are much more accustomed to, as poet Billy Collins once put it, "tie the poem to a chair with rope / and torture a confession out of it." Whatever emotions the poem might stir in our students, we perhaps imply to them, are their business, and don't belong in the classroom. Stick to the facts (or formulae, or concepts, or whatever the technical tools of our discipline might be). But theories of intrinsic motivation tell us that if we want students to learn the material as deeply as possible, we have to *first* help students see the ways in which our course material connects meaningfully to our lives, or can help us solve problems or enrich our futures. Only after they have seen and understood this will they take the time to become genuinely interested, as Kaufman's student puts it, "in what each work really *means*"—which should then stir their interest in the formal tools of disciplinary analysis that will help them find that meaning.

I suggested earlier that fostering intrinsic motivation in our students can happen in three ways: connecting the questions of the course to questions the students already have; challenging the students with questions or problems that you can help them see as fascinating and important; and engaging them with authentic assessments. Let's elaborate on each of these three conditions by considering Kaufman's course in a bit more detail.

Undoubtedly the conversations that Kaufman's students have with the residents of the correctional center help them see the connections between their own lives and the classic works of Russian literature. The special genius of this course is that Kaufman asks his students to design conversations that will highlight the links between Russian literature and the lives of the residents—as they do so, the students are simultaneously thinking about and seeing connections between the literature and their *own* lives. This should not come as too much of a surprise, since the residents and the students are not too far apart in age and hence share some commonalities. Both groups are in a kind of waiting period before adulthood will really begin, and so they share a particular interest in what the future will hold for them, and how the forces of the world will shape and mold their adult lives. When the students come to see the works of the great Russian writers as offering them insights and ideas into what that process will entail, and how they can best negotiate it, they become intrinsically motivated to learn more about what those authors might have to teach them.

This becomes especially evident when you read the comments of students who have taken the course, which Kaufman has been gathering for his own study of the effectiveness of his approach to teaching literature. The Russian works they were reading and teaching to the residents, one student said, "covered the deepest questions of humanity: Who are we? Why are we here? What is our place in life? How should we act with other people? What does death mean? That's a big one. All of those kinds of questions that everybody meditates on. These are questions that apply to everybody." Another student likened the difference between Kaufman's approach to literature and the approach she encountered in most literature courses to the difference between theoretical and applied mathematics: "If you can have calculus and applied calculus, I think . . . this class is applied literature. You're applying it to your life. The personal aspect is something you don't ever get in English classes. You're not expected or ever requested to compare it [the literature] to your life to see if you could relate to it." Taken metaphorically, that analogy seems like an apt one to me in thinking about this approach to fostering intrinsic motivation. While every course we teach might have a theoretical or pure side to it, connecting to the questions that students bring to our courses means thinking about the "applied" nature of our disciplines and our courses. What do our courses have to offer that will help students answer the questions that they already have—whether those questions are about mortality, or politics, or race, or the chemicals in our food? How can we design our courses in ways that will give students a clear vision of these applications? Kaufman has approached this challenge in a unique way—by asking his students to think about the applications of the course material to the lives of the residents, he helps them see its applications to their own lives as well.

But the course also fosters intrinsic motivation in that it presents a difficult and fascinating challenge to the students, one that forces them to work together in order to achieve their goals. Prior to the registration period for the coming semester's courses, Kaufman holds an information session on campus about Books Behind Bars, inviting students to come and learn about what they will be doing in the course. Students know well in advance of the course that they will be responsible for guiding conversations about Russian literature with the residents of a juvenile correctional center. This real-world experience looms above them from the moment they enter the course, and guides and inspires all of their learning. One student noted, in her comment about the course, that the prospect of facing this difficult challenge brought the students together as a group, as well as heightening their interest in the course:

> we were all in such a new position and none of us knew what it was going to be like. So, you were naturally on adrenaline, excited when you were talking with people about it. And that makes you feel closer to people when you're that excited. And you're naturally going to be more open with people. And you're all going in with the same kind of fears and vulnerabilities and that bonds people faster, I think. The idea of being so vulnerable and not knowing what's gonna happen. You're naturally more willing to talk to people and to open up. It's a kind of, 'You're all in this together,' feeling.

This student offers a fascinating insight into the way in which a challenging academic task can help not only motivate the students, but also draw them closer to one another, as they realize that they can rely on one another for both emotional and intellectual support. Their shared purpose, and their uncertainty in the face of a large and unstructured problem, creates an immediate sense of cohesion among the group.

Bain's theories on motivation suggest that intrinsically motivating questions we pose to the students have to be authentic ones—they cannot be questions to which we already have the answers, and toward which we slowly lead students in a step-by-step process. They have to be precisely the kind of unstructured, open-ended problems or questions that we all address in our own research. Such questions can be posed to the students through individual assignments, but Kaufman really poses these questions through the entire structure of his course: Can the great works of Russian literature help provide insights or guidance into the lives of these troubled teens? If so, how can Kaufman's students help the residents see and understand—

and perhaps even act upon—those insights? Ultimately, how can these college students—many of whom are coming from positions of great relative privilege—make a positive difference in the lives of these juvenile offenders?

Bain's work also suggests that if we are asking students to grapple with authentic, open-ended questions or problems, we have to give them the freedom and autonomy to follow those questions wherever they may lead—just as our own research questions lead us into a maze of unpredictable places at times, as we follow false leads and dead ends and promising notions, often ending up in places that we could never have predicted at the outset. Kaufman accomplishes this by setting a difficult challenge before his students, and then stepping back and becoming a facilitator who helps the students meet that challenge. He provides readings for them in Russian literature and in pedagogy, guiding them in conversations about how they can best meet the challenge of working with the residents. But the students have the responsibility for creating their lesson plans, for holding the conversations, and for following the paths that are opened up by those conversations. In the words of one student, "It was pretty evident from the beginning that it was going to be the professor laying the groundwork and us doing most of the work. And I think that was pretty consistent. When we went into class we really expected that it was going to be us doing most of the work, which was good. We really had ownership of that class." Their ownership of the course means that each small group conversation between students and residents looks a little different from the others: some students plan more structured activities with the stories or poems they have read while others seek to foster more informal conversations. In every case, though, the students have the primary responsibility for determining how they will meet the challenge that Kaufman has set for them.

Whether you are designing a course that addresses the questions the students bring, or posing them challenging questions that you hope will intrigue and inspire them—or both—the final essential element in fostering intrinsic motivation is the use of authentic assessments. Authentic assessments allow students to respond to the questions in ways that allow them to show what they have learned, rather than to check off boxes or jump through hoops. We will cover this notion in more detail in the next chapter, but for now we can get a glimpse of it in Kaufman's assignment for his course. Throughout the semester, the students are regularly writing journal entries and other shorter essays that describe what they are learning from their experiences preparing for and talking with the residents. At the end of the semester, they compile those writings into a "Learning Portfolio," which they use as the basis for a final reflective essay on the course. In describing the purpose of the essay on his syllabus, Kaufman explains that they should analyze their Learning Portfolio in order to see how it "reflect[s] changes in your thinking and/or writing about literature, life, your education as a whole, about you as a learner and as a person, about the way you understand yourself and others, etc. In other words, you and your learning experience [in the course] are the subject of this essay." What I think really matters about this assignment is the way in which it invites the students to reflect upon and document their own learning. Just as Kaufman gives students autonomy in terms of how they meet the challenge of the course—teaching Russian literature to the residents—so he gives them autonomy in thinking about how to best demonstrate to him what they have learned in the course. Authenticity in this context does not mean that the assignment replicates something you might find outside of the classroom, in the "real world"; it means instead that students must draw from themselves and their own experiences in order to prepare the work they submit for evaluation.

I want to finish my analysis of Books Behind Bars by pointing out that, of course, Kaufman's learning portfolios are literally an uncheatable assignment—much of the writing for the Learning Portfolio comes from in-class writing assignments, and students must write their reflective essays about their experiences with the residents, which Kaufman has spent the semester observing. Those portfolios, in addition to the work they do in helping to foster intrinsic motivation, represent the ideal example of what I call a *grounded assessment*.[13] You will not find a more effective means of eliminating cheating in your courses than grounding your assessments, by which I mean that you design assessments that are unique to each specific course you teach, each semester. While that might sound like a time-consuming nightmare, it does not have to be. Kaufman's course, by its very nature, creates grounded assessments because each semester his students will have a new set of conversations with a new set of residents. Since he has supervised and observed those conversations, students cannot simply fabricate their learning portfolio or find similar experiences online—they must speak from and engage with the unique experiences they had in the course in that semester. Courses that depend upon community service learning, or any kind of major event or interaction with others, lend themselves automatically to grounded assessments—perhaps our best defense against cheating.

But grounded assessments don't actually require community service learning, or building your course around visits to a juvenile correctional center, or any other conceptual overhaul of your teaching. You can use highly cheating-resistant grounded assessments in any course with just a little bit of creative thinking. For the past several years I have been hearing from students about a colleague who was grounding her assessments in unique and fascinating ways. Sarah Cavanagh is an assistant professor at

Assumption College who has quickly built a reputation as an outstanding teacher in high demand. Cavanagh's research interests focus on the interaction of psychological and biological processes in healthy and disrupted emotion regulation; her areas of teaching focus are motivation and emotion; social, cognitive, and affective neuroscience; and a multidisciplinary approach to teaching abnormal psychology. Like all of us here on campus, she teaches a mix of lower- and upper-division courses, with a regular suite of introductory courses in her discipline each year—in her case, the general psychology course taken by many freshman for a general education requirement. I asked Cavanagh if she would show me examples of some of the grounded assessments she uses in her courses. The ones she provided for me helped me to see more clearly the different ways in which faculty in any discipline, in even the most conventional types of courses and teaching formats, can ground their assessments. In the examples that I will give from Cavanagh's courses, you will see assignments or exam questions that are grounded in the unique experience of the course in four different ways:

1. *Time.* Students connect course content to events, conversations, trends, or research they experience uniquely within the confines of that semester.
2. *Place.* Students connect to something in the local community, whether that means their dorm, their campus, or the city in which their institution is located.
3. *Personal.* Students consider how course content shapes or could be used to understand a specific experience in their lives.
4. *Interdisciplinary.* Students draw connections not only between your course content and other disciplines they have studied, but especially between your course and other specific

courses they have taken, or co-curricular activities like on-campus lectures, performances, and other learning-oriented events.

Let's consider an example of each of these kinds of grounded assessments from Sarah Cavanagh's courses.[14]

Time. In Cavanagh's introductory course in General Psychology, she wants students to develop basic media literacy in the subject, and learn how to evaluate the accuracy of reporting on psychological topics in the press. To help accomplish that goal, she gives them this assignment:

> Find a recent (i.e., posted in the last few months) popular media account describing the findings of a psychological study. Good sources include the *New York Times,* "the body odd" on msnbc, and *TIME Magazine* online. Using the school library's website, find the original research article the media account is describing. Write a 1–3 page letter to the editor evaluating the popular media piece. If their account was thorough and accurate, describe why. If their account was inaccurate, over-simplified, or different in emphasis than the original research article, describe why. Conclude with a statement about the influence of popular media on public perceptions of psychology, and the importance of holding the popular media accountable for accurate portrayals.

Such an assignment obviously cannot be shared from semester to semester, since the students have to engage with a very recent piece of research. The concluding paragraph she describes might leave itself open to plagiarism, but the heart of the assignment is one that students will have to engage in afresh every semester. As effectively as this assignment deters potential plagiarism, I find it even more impressive in its ability to help students see the currency and relevance of what they are learning in Cavanagh's course by asking them to notice how this academic discipline manifests itself on a daily basis in the media that surrounds them. The assignment also encourages students to see themselves as members of a scholarly discipline who are charged with evaluating the work of others who are thinking or writing about their subject matter.

Place. Cavanagh's place-based assignment, used in an upper-level psychology course, shares elements of Kaufman's course in the way it asks students to engage with and serve the local community. Supervising this assignment over the past two years, she told me, has been one of the most satisfying experiences of her career. Students in her Physiological Psychology course give a group presentation on a topic in neuroscience. But instead of just asking them to step to the front of the room and do the usual PowerPoint song and dance, she presents them with a much more challenging and innovative assignment:

> Working with several other students in a group, you will design a 5–10 minute lesson plan for 5th graders covering some aspect of basic brain anatomy or function. You will submit draft and final lesson plans, and we will hold a "dress rehearsal" of these lesson plans in class. During National Brain Awareness Week in March, you and your group members will present these lesson plans in a local elementary school.

As Cavanagh acknowledged when she sent me this example, students can undoubtedly still get their information from online sources, and potentially plagiarize parts of it. But even if they do this, as she also pointed out, "they still have to modify them to fit the age group and the time frame, and the bulk of the work is in the practicing, dress rehearsal, and leading the students the day of the event." And, she added, as a bonus, "having to perform in unusual circumstances also seems to lead to a sharp reduction in 'phoning it in' presentations—the students are really engaged and enthusiastic." An assessment like this one pulls disciplinary questions from the ether and drops them directly into the community in which our students are living, helping them see its relevance to their lives today—and, of course, making it much more difficult for them to disengage from the assignment and complete it dishonestly.

Personal. Research on human memory from cognitive theorists points convincingly to the fact that creating personal connections to knowledge helps create deeper learning. In *The Seven Sins of Memory,* Daniel Schacter, a neuropsychologist at Harvard, notes that "numerous experiments have shown that when we encode new information by relating it to the self, subsequent memory for that information improves compared to other types of encoding."[15] Our memories, Schacter theorizes, prefer to hang on longer to information for which we can see some obvious personal relevance.[16] In Cavanagh's upper-level course on Motivation and Emotion, she gives her students the opportunity to make such personal connections to the course material with the following essay assignment:

> What are the primary forces that shape your behavior? Which of the topics we've covered have the most relevance for your daily experiences and choices? Choose a particular instance/anecdote in which there were strong motivational influences on your behavior and tie in the motivational forces at play in your life with the relevant concepts and topics covered in class. Examples could be a major life decision, your struggles to break a particular habit, your work to reach a particular goal, etc.

As Cavanagh pointed out to me herself, this assignment also does not necessarily preclude cheating, since it would be possible to fabricate an incident or grab someone else's off the internet. But as we all know about human beings, and as you probably have learned from the occasional experience you've had sitting next to a chatty stranger on the bus or standing in line at the grocery store, people like talking about themselves and analyzing their own experiences. So the students should likely be more motivated to write this assignment honestly, and use it to understand their own personal experiences more deeply, than they would if they were asked to analyze a hypothetical incident or some textbook example. That motivation, along with the connections they build between the course material and their personal experiences, should help reduce cheating and deepen learning.[17]

Interdisciplinary. Four years ago on my own campus we began offering to our first-year students the option to take linked interdisciplinary courses on topics developed by faculty members from two different disciplines. The students took the two courses separately, but the faculty worked together throughout the year to ensure that assessments and course content fed into each other. Many faculty who taught within these linkages—including Cavanagh and a colleague in chemistry—developed assignments that required students to draw upon their specific interdisciplinary pairing. Here is an essay question that Cavanagh proposed to her students on an exam at the end of the semester in the General Psychology course that was linked with an introductory chemistry course:

> Imagine you are home for Christmas break when your mother pulls you aside and tells you that she is really concerned with your younger sister's eating patterns. She has been alternating between cycles of eating lots of junk food and then over-restricting her eating by following one of a number of fad diets. Using the information we covered in class regarding personal and societal

influences on eating behavior, what you learned in your linked
chemistry course regarding the effects of fad diets on your body,
and the information provided by the nutrition speaker at our extracurricular Q&A event, give your mother and sister some advice.

What I found especially compelling about this assignment was
the way that it required the student to draw not only upon the
interdisciplinary pairing but also on a linked co-curricular event.
Drawing co-curricular events like those into the assessments for
the course provides one more assurance that students are doing
work for your uniquely structured learning experience instead of
relying on material developed by students (or professional researchers who prey on students) for a more generic learning experience. If you do not have a connected-course structure like
the one on my campus, you can still create unique interdisciplinary groundings by asking students to link course material to co-
curricular activities on campus, or to any other required courses
you know they have taken at your institution.

Here we are at the close of the chapter, and you might find yourself surprised at how little space I have devoted to cheating, the
explicit subject matter of this book. The chapters in Part II are
designed to provide guidance in modifying your teaching in
ways that reduce cheating by increasing learning. Students who
want to learn, and who have been given all of the tools they
need to learn, have no need to cheat. So my goal in this part of
the book is to help you understand what the experts tell us
about how to motivate students to learn, and how to give them
the tools they need to learn. Remember, though, that we are not
taking on the universe in that respect: we are focused on the elements of a learning environment that research tells us can also—

in addition to increasing or decreasing learning—induce or reduce cheating.

In this chapter we have considered strategies designed to increase intrinsic motivation, which I would argue is the most important feature of a learning environment in terms of its potential to reduce cheating. We saw how Andy Kaufman seeks to inspire intrinsic motivation with the large and fascinating questions he poses to his students, and we saw how both Kaufman and Sarah Cavanagh do so with assessments that are grounded in the lives and unique learning experiences of their students. Kaufman and Cavanagh represent two ends of a spectrum of potential course revisions you might make, from restructuring your course to modifying your specific assessments. In both cases, though, the principles are the same: connect your course material to the questions and interests that students bring to your classroom; challenge and fascinate them with authentic questions and problems that you bring to them; and ask them to respond to those questions and challenges with unique, grounded assessments.

Those principles should be able to guide the work of any faculty member seeking to foster intrinsic motivation in her students, no matter how large or introductory the course they may be teaching—and, hence, no matter how restricted they may feel in their ability to incorporate community service elements like Kaufman's or more personalized assignments like Cavanagh's. Even if you are ultimately responsible for preparing students for some external exam, or covering some basic survey material, or fulfilling a general education requirement, don't begin there. Don't write course descriptions that describe what you will be covering, foreground them on the syllabus, and jump right into that coverage on the first day. Spend a little time thinking about the *questions* of the course—the fascinating questions that intrigue you about the course material, and the questions that might connect to what motivates your students in their lives right now. Highlight those questions everywhere you can: on your syllabus, in class, and in your assignments and exams. Find ways to remind your students, as often as possible, that what your course has to offer them is more than just the extrinsic reward of a grade.

5

LEARNING FOR MASTERY

We commonly use the phrase "jumping through hoops" to speak of required performances that seem divorced from any meaningful context—I used it in the last chapter to describe assignments that are unlikely to inspire intrinsic motivation. In this chapter I want to take that familiar phrase and build it into a metaphor designed to introduce the basic difference between a performance-oriented classroom environment and a mastery-oriented one. Remember that the first cheating-inducing factor we encountered, in both our historical survey and the social science literature, was a strong emphasis on performance. When students place greater emphasis on performance than learning, they are more likely to cheat; and when the learning or task-completion environment places greater emphasis on performance than on skill or task mastery, human beings are more likely to cheat. Athletics provides an easy arena in which to understand the difference between performance and mastery orientations, so we will spend a few hypothetical pages in that realm before we turn back to higher education.

Imagine you have spent a few months teaching a group of young people to improve their skills in athleticism and dexterity. At the end of your time with them, you bring them to a gymnasium in order to allow them to demonstrate their newly developed skills, and to evaluate them on how much they have improved over the course of their training. In a performance-oriented classroom, you would ask each student in that gymnasium to show off her skills by making a single jump through a hoop. That jump might certainly tell you whether the student has reached a basic level of athletic ability. But for some students, that single required performance might not give you a true picture of their abilities: a student who was sick that day, for example, or another who suffered from weak ankles, despite solid athletic ability in other ways, might fail at that one particular task. So the test would provide limited—and possibly flawed—data about the athletic ability of your students.

Now imagine instead that you brought those students into a gymnasium that was filled with stations designed to allow your athletes to demonstrate a variety of skills: hoops for jumping, bars for pull-ups, a track for sprinting, barbells for weight-lifting, and so on. I am sure most of us would agree that asking the athletes to engage with as many of these stations as possible, and evaluating their overall performance on multiple stations, would provide a better and more accurate depiction of their true athletic ability than the simple hoop-jumping performance. But now imagine an even more radical innovation. Instead of simply pointing students to five stations and asking them to complete a required performance at each one, you brought each student into the gymnasium, walked them one by one through each of a dozen or more stations, and then said: "Now show me what you can do." Each athlete would then have the option of selecting the stations that were most conducive to helping you see the athletic skills he had developed; you might select some minimum number of stations that each one had to complete, and pick one or two required ones, but beyond that it would be completely up to the athlete to show mastery of the skills that have been taught. As long as you have designed the stations in such a way that the athletes could not simply spend their training period focusing on one or two skills that would see them through all stations, this environment would no doubt give you the best and most accurate depiction of what your athletes were capable of, allowing them to show off their particular strengths while demonstrating some basic level of competence in a set of skills.

It might strike you that such a gymnasium sounds like a benign version of the one in which contestants train for their mortal combat in Suzanne Collins's *Hunger Games* novels. As you may recall, those novels (and their film versions) pit two dozen young men and women from impoverished districts of a dystopian world against each other in a fight to the death for the viewing pleasure of wealthy residents of the capital city. Prior to entering the combat arena, the contestants spend several days in a gymnasium that features multiple stations dedicated to various survival skills, from handling weapons to starting fires or identifying edible plants. The contestants are free to choose which skills they want to learn, and wander from station to station according to their interests and abilities. At the completion of their training, they select which skill they will demonstrate to the arbiters of the games. Their demonstration of this skill will help determine their ranking in the competition—a high-pressure performance, no doubt. But that performance tests the candidates on a skill that they have chosen to master, and which best suits their particular talents and abilities. The heroine of the novel wisely chooses to avoid stations devoted to weight training or single-handed combat and instead focuses on archery and basic survival skills—decisions which, in the tidy world of the novel, turn out to be instrumental in helping her win the games.[1]

In both *The Hunger Games* and our benign hypothetical example, the learners *do* have to engage in a performance that is assessed by an evaluator. You will not find me arguing here that we can or should remove that element from the educational process. But in both cases the performance has become secondary to the learning objective. Rather than the *end itself,* as I suspect students often think about our projects or exams, it has become only the *means* to the end—it serves as one possible opportunity among many to demonstrate their mastery of a skill or a body of knowledge. Our hypothetical athletes know that a weak performance in hoop-jumping can be outweighed by a solid performance on the pull-up bars, and that they can all find some ways in order to demonstrate their general athleticism. Protagonist Katniss Everdeen and her fellow combatants in *The Hunger Games* know that they can impress their judges with their survival skills through fire-building and plant identification just as well as they can through wielding swords and maces. When learners of any kind have multiple ways to demonstrate their knowledge or skill, or are able to choose the types of performances that will best allow them to showcase their knowledge or skill, or are able to make multiple attempts at a performance, the emphasis shifts away from the specific performance and falls more heavily on their mastery of what they must learn. So a learning environment (such as a college classroom) that emphasizes mastery over performance should establish a clear learning objective for the students and then give them choices in how they could best meet that learning objective, as well as providing them with multiple and perhaps even repeated opportunities to do so. Andy Kaufman's course, in which students write journal entries each week and then compile their own best work into a learning portfolio, represents one excellent example of that kind of assessment strategy. By contrast, a performance-oriented learning environment places the emphasis on students doing well on the specific performances established by the evaluator. This type of classroom lends itself not only to cheating but also to students focusing on things like test-taking strategies (i.e., to guess or not guess on a multiple choice exam) instead of actually learning the material.

Contrary to what you might now be expecting, I have not asked either Katniss Everdeen or Suzanne Collins to serve as our guide for the creation of a mastery-oriented classroom. Instead, I have asked that favor of John Boyer, a faculty member in the Geography department at Virginia Tech who teaches a World Regions class with an impressive mastery orientation to around 2,670 students every spring semester.

Yes, you read that correctly. 2,670 students.

These are students sitting in a classroom, I should add, not watching his lectures online. He considers himself limited to that number of students only by the size of the auditorium where he holds his classes; if he could find a bigger auditorium, he would happily teach even larger classes—and he would have no trouble doing so, since his classes are filled to capacity and many students have to wait for several semesters before they are able to gain one of the (many) coveted seats in Boyer's lecture hall. Boyer gained his fame in the academic community when a reporter for the *Chronicle of Higher Education* wrote a profile of this incredibly popular World Regions class in April of 2012. The story focused primarily on the eye-popping numbers of students who took Boyer's class, and on the implications that his ability to attract such numbers might have for the future of the profession. The article includes statistics about the increasing reliance on large courses in state universities, and also includes a comment from Peter E. Doolittle, director of Virginia Tech's Center for Instructional Development and Educational Research, who notes that, in tough budgetary times, such massive courses may become more and more popular: "They're not going anywhere . . . We're better off learning how to teach well in large classes, rather than trying to avoid them." Most of the article focuses on precisely that issue: how does Boyer manage to teach well in such a large class?[2]

When I first saw the article headline, I had the same question. And, like many faculty members who commented on the article, I was skeptical at first that much learning could take place in such an outsized classroom. I wondered whether Boyer was simply a great showman, one who could give dazzling lectures or multimedia performances, more of a performer than a teacher. But what really caught my eye in the *Chronicle* article, and encouraged me to dig more deeply into his teaching, was the following paragraph:

> Boyer describes his course as an "Intro to the Planet" that brings "the average completely uninformed American" up to speed on world issues. His approach? Decentralize the rigid class format by recreating assessment as a gamelike system in which students earn points for completing assignments of their choosing from many options (1,050 points earns an A, and no tasks, not even exams, are required). Saturate students with Facebook and Twitter updates (some online pop quizzes are announced only on social media). Keep the conversation going with online office hours.[3]

I tend to respond to any new-fangled teaching approaches or technologies with caution, knowing that sometimes "innovative" technologies or methods turn out to be nothing more than expensive or time-consuming replications of more traditional or conventional approaches that still work perfectly well. So while my eyes rolled a little bit at buzzwords like "decentralize" and "gamelike," I was intrigued enough by the description of an assessment system with multiple options to hunt down his online course materials, which are plentiful, and explore a little further. In what follows I will draw upon multiple sources, including Boyer's syllabus and statements of educational philosophy (all available online), as well as email and video interviews I conducted with him about the course and his teaching.

Boyer describes his World Regions course on his syllabus as one designed "to broaden and strengthen the individual's interest in the world at large; to consider how/where/why physical and cultural forces shape and define the earth we live on."[4] Within that broadly defined objective, he breaks down the student learning objectives into a typical triad of skills (such as the ability to critically evaluate media sources), knowledge (such as basic physical characteristics of major world regions) and beliefs or attitudes (empathy with diverse global perspectives). The bulk of his syllabus focuses on explaining to students the structure and *raison d'etre* of his assessment system, as well as the details of the individual assignment and exam options. I want to begin my analysis of Boyer's course with the section of his syllabus that presents and explains his assessment system to his students:

> This is a radical, experimental course when it comes to grading, and I hope you embrace and enjoy this change. If you don't, then you should bail out now, not later. Instead of having a set amount of mandatory activities that you are required to do and then assessing your grade from your performance, I am going to provide a host of opportunities for you to earn points towards your grade, thus allowing you to choose your path according to your interests and skills.
>
> It's a "create your fate" grade: you choose what you want to work on, and keep earning points doing different activities until you achieve the grade you desire. Are you an excellent test-taker? Then take lots of tests. Not good at taking exams? Then do alternative written or film viewing assignments to earn your points. I would suggest mixing it up and doing a little of everything to cover all your bases and ensure you get enough points to get the grade of your desires.

In alignment with precisely what I think makes this assessment system so effective for learning, Boyer notes that he wants to shift the emphasis away from "your performance," and instead give the students "opportunities." This is not the way that I suspect most students, and perhaps even most faculty, think about their presentations or exams or papers. But if we want to create a mastery-oriented classroom—one that both increases learning and reduces the incentive to cheat—this may be precisely the way we *should* think about it. Assessments present *opportunities* for students to demonstrate how well they have achieved the learning objectives for the course; they are not the learning objectives themselves.

Boyer's description of the course options in the second paragraph, I should note, might overstate slightly the wide-open nature of the student's options in the course. No single type of assignment or exam will enable the students to earn enough points to achieve a passing grade in the course. As he suggests to them in the second paragraph, they have to take advantage of several different types of opportunities in order to pass the class. The total points available throughout the semester come out to around 1,500; anything above 1,050 earns the students an A, and they need at least 730 points to pass. The three major exams in the course total up to 350, so even if students are excellent test-takers, they still need to engage in a few other activities in order to pass the course. A student who loves film and takes advantage of the opportunities the course provides to attend and write responses to film viewings would be able to earn only 300 points from those assessments. This is worth pointing out because I can foresee some skepticism from readers about the way in which this system might allow students not only to play to their strengths but also to avoid assessments in some area that you believe is critical for students to know in your course or discipline. A carefully crafted assessment system using this model can achieve the best of both worlds: giving students plenty of opportunities, but also ensuring that they have to engage with whatever you believe are the most critical components of your course.

When I asked Boyer to explain how and why he first adopted this mastery orientation in the course, he said it did not come to him in one grand epiphany; instead, over the course of a few years, three gradually coalescing factors pushed him to try it out for the first time in the spring of 2011, when he had only 550 students in the course. The first main driving force in pushing him to structure the course in this way was the logistical complexity of running a course with close to 3,000 students. As he explained to me in our video interview, trying to mandate any single form of assessment for that many students, even a very conventional one, becomes almost impossible in the face of such large numbers: "The standard operating procedure of having a midterm and final exam was just not workable—it became more trouble than it was worth for all parties involved: me, the TA team, the students. When you bump the numbers up that high, you might end up with 200–300 people who have a very good excuse to miss an exam." We all know the complexities involved when we are trying to schedule an alternate exam for students who have to miss an exam for a legitimate excuse, such as a death in the family. Imagine trying to deal with such complexities when you have 200–300 students to reschedule, and you are trying to provide reasonable alternatives to each of them. And then imagine that you want to incorporate outside events, such as screening international films, and need to find times that would be available to almost 3,000 students. It just doesn't work—or it works at the expense of many dozens of hours spent by Boyer and his teaching assistants trying to juggle schedules.[5]

A second reason Boyer adduced for the system was that, in his words, "I had so many cool assignments I wanted to try!" Whether you are communicating with John Boyer by email or video, and I would imagine in person, almost everything comes with an exclamation point. He seems to possess boundless energy, as well as boundless enthusiasm for his course, his teaching, and his students. He also has a passionate interest in educational technology, and so each year he adopts or tweaks assessments that push himself and his students in new directions. In the spring of 2012, for example, he first tried out an assessment form using the social networking site Twitter. Students who opted for this assignment were given a choice of one of eighty-five world leaders to impersonate on a specially designated Twitter network for John's course. They had to post tweets from that world leader at least twice a day, offering information on their location, their activities for the day, and any interactions they had with other world leaders. The students were responsible for consulting news sources, which provided the information they needed for their tweets, and then they used that information to create the words and persona of the leaders they had been assigned. For two tweets per day, or at least sixty per semester, students could earn up to 200 points toward their final course grade. Boyer's interests in new and different forms of assessment allowed him to add such assignments to an already crowded curriculum—more assessments than any individual student could complete during a single semester. The multi-choice assessment system gave the students more options between assignments like the Twitter exercise and more conventional forms of assessment, such as quizzes and exams.

But the third and most important reason Boyer presented for adopting this system was the very basic pedagogical one that, in his estimation, it helps motivate the students to learn. "My first priority in teaching," he explained to me in our video interview, "is getting people interested and inspired, and wanting to learn more on their own time—even after the class is over, I want them to be inspired to continue learning. In my mind, the best way to do that is to get them doing things that they are genuinely interested in doing, in the avenues in which they learn best." So, as he points out, and as we all probably know from experience, some students claim to be poor test-takers. Whether we should accept that self-definition or not (and some learning theorists would argue that we should not), a student who has that self-definition may view a learning experience that uses nothing but tests as assessments as a negative or intimidating one—even if that student has an inherent or intrinsic interest in the subject matter. Another student might love the study of politics and geography but have little interest in their depiction in films; and that student might find himself equally turned off in a class that had required film viewings and responses. In Boyer's class, students are free to choose the form of assessment that they see as most interesting and most conducive to their showing him what and how much they have learned. So instead of the assessments looming over their heads as potentially intimidating or demotivating moments in the course, they become—as Boyer describes them on his syllabus—*opportunities* to demonstrate learning.

I want to dig a little deeper, with the help of pedagogical theory on mastery learning, to see how and why Boyer's multi-choice assessment system may help students develop the kind of intrinsic motivation and lifelong interest in his subject matter that he describes above. In a statement of teaching philosophy on his website, under the title of "New Educational Approaches," Boyer explains that his assessment system provides a means to individualize the course experience for every student in the (very large) room:

> Students in the World Regions class come from diverse backgrounds (with approximately 80 countries represented), with different levels of knowledge and experiences, driven by differing motivations and maturity. As the class size and student diversity increases, it becomes increasingly difficult for instructors to devise a single exam or assignment to challenge and assess such a

group . . . the goal [of the assessment system] is to create an individualized and unique experience for each student, despite the fact that they are participating in a class of 2750 students.

Boyer sees his role as creating an "individualized and unique learning experience for each student"—a difficult enough challenge even in a twenty-student senior seminar; for an instructor to do so with close to 3,000 students in a single semester seems hopelessly quixotic. The default mode, in the face of such a challenge, would be to jump every student through the same set of hoops and hope for the best.[6]

Boyer has chosen an alternate route. Since it's impossible for the instructor to create unique learning experiences for so many students, the instructor *doesn't* do so: instead, he gives the students the autonomy to create their own individualized learning experiences through his multi-choice assessment system. In doing so, he has oriented the course away from one-size-fits all performance and toward students determining the best ways for them to demonstrate their mastery of the course's learning objectives. The literature on how to construct a course with a mastery orientation would affirm the wisdom of Boyer's assessment system in that respect. Susan Ambrose and her colleagues, in *How Learning Works,* note that providing "flexibility and control" counts as one of the major strategies that help orient students toward learning over performance goals. To develop a mastery learning orientation, they suggest, "allow students to choose among options and make choices that are consistent with their goals and the activities that they value."[7] Exam-takers get to take exams, in other words, and social media users get to complete assignments on Twitter.

A research report published in a 2005 issue of the *Journal of Marketing Education* points out another key way in which the assessment system we see in Boyer's class can help promote mastery learning. "Providing numerous opportunities to practice, learn, and master the task at hand," the authors of the study suggest, "will enhance intrinsic motivation by developing students' competencies."[8] Intrinsic motivation and mastery learning are closely linked. When students approach a learning task from intrinsic motivation, they are more likely to engage in mastery learning than performance learning. So how do you give students "numerous" opportunities to practice, learn, and master a task? Again we can look to Boyer. The highest possible point opportunity in Boyer's class comes from the weekly textbook quizzes, which he posts online every Tuesday. Students can earn a total of 400 points if they ace all of those quizzes. And, true to the mastery orientation of Boyer's overall assessment strategy, students can take them as many times as they like, until they get them right. Here is how he presents them to his students on the syllabus (using the occasionally colorful language you will find in everything he writes):

> These quizzes are open-notes, open-book, open-website and can be taken as many times as you like. In other words, keep taking the damn thing until you get a 100% on it. Each weekly quiz will be posted on Tuesday after class and will be available until the following Tuesday before class begins, when it will be replaced by the new quiz for that week.

Nothing says mastery—seriously, nothing at all—like telling a learner that they get to keep practicing and trying until they get it right.

Finally, in an older but thorough analysis of the research in this area, the educational psychologist Carole Ames reviews the "the structures of the classroom environment that lead to a mastery goal orientation."[9] Two of the specific features that she identifies as essential to a mastery classroom are clearly present in the assessment structure used by Boyer. First, she notes that tasks which "give students a sense of control over either the process or product" are more likely to produce mastery orientations.[10] This may be, she points out, because the variety of tasks and the individual paths that students carve through them render it more difficult for students to engage in competitive comparisons of their scores on any given assessment—behavior that would orient them more toward performance than learning. Second, displacing some of the authority from the teacher to the student, in terms of the tasks they complete in the course, helps push students toward mastery orientations. "Allowing students to have a say in establishing priorities in task completion," as Ames describes it,[11] sounds like a pretty accurate description of John Boyer's classroom.

Ames's review helps clarify an important reason that a multi-choice assessment structure like Boyer's pushes students away from performance orientations: it directs them away from constant focus on their exam or assignment performance *in comparison to others in the class.* Learners who may be doing very well in learning the material, but who perform poorly on an assessment compared to their peers, may become discouraged and unmotivated to continue trying to learn. Whenever I give exams back in my classes, I am always surprised to see how willing and even interested the students are to compare their scores with one another. In smaller classes, in which the students are very comfortable with me and one another, I have even had students call their exam scores out loud when I handed them back, noting how well they did in comparison to their nearby peers. Imagine a student who has worked very hard to achieve an 85 percent on an exam, an excellent score for her specific capacities on that exam in that class. If she happens to be sitting next to a high-capability student who has aced the exam, and is not shy about broadcasting it, suddenly her remarkable achievement will no longer feel quite so remarkable—and that may, in turn, discourage her from working quite so hard the next time around, since her best effort still fell fifteen percentage points short of her vocal neighbor. Grade competition and comparisons push students toward performance orientations; allowing each student to create their own unique assessment structure de-emphasizes both competition and comparison.

Finally, in his description of his educational philosophy, Boyer points out another way in which the performance emphasis of traditional grading systems actually may serve to discourage learners. In many types of grading systems, Boyer points out correctly, "from the very first day of class, a student has an A+, and then instructors give the students a series of assignments and tests that serve to take points away from them when they mark items as incorrect. Every type of assessment, such as a paper or an exam, is viewed not as a chance to gain points but rather as an opportunity to lose them." A student operating under such a system sees nothing but bleeding points or grades from the first assessment of the semester. Such a course sets a standard of perfection for the required performances, and almost every student performance will fall short of that standard by at least a little. But when you turn that system upside down, as Boyer has done, the emphasis of the course shifts away from required group performances and toward the individualized opportunities for the students to demonstrate their mastery of the course content. Boyer concludes his explanation of his assessment system using an athletic metaphor akin to the one with which this chapter began: he compares performance-oriented systems to hurdle-jumping, and contrasts that with what students can experience in a mastery-oriented system: "This method is intended to motivate students with challenge, choice, control, and curiosity instead of presenting them hurdles to be over-come." Or, put in the terms with which I opened this chapter, such a method allows students to follow their specific strengths and inclinations in order to demonstrate their mastery of the course content instead of simply asking them to keep jumping through hoops all semester long.

As you might expect, making changes like these to a course assessment system—just like making any kind of substantive change to a course—creates the potential for new problems, or problems that might not exist in other types of systems. In Boyer's course—as I suspect would be the case in any choice-assessment method—the clear problem each student must face comes in the form of procrastination. Students who wait too long to begin their unique package of assessments, and who don't bother to take and retake the quizzes, may find themselves facing the end of the semester with no possibility of passing the course. As Boyer explained it to me in our interview, "Because it's so flexible, and so open, and there are so many options, there is a propensity to put everything off until the end. There are students who get lost in the sauce." The propensity of students to get "lost in the sauce" is exacerbated in a course of nearly 3,000 students, since it's more difficult for Boyer and his teach-ing assistants to keep track of the progress of individual students.

I asked Boyer what he did, and what other instructors could do, in order to help students avoid falling into the sauce and finding themselves stuck there, with too few options, at the end of the semester. "You do have to absolutely stress to all students that it's on their shoulders," he replied. "You have to do this from day one; you need persistent explanations on the syllabus and regular announcements on the syllabus and via email about how many points they should have, or how many assignments they should have done." At the end of his explanation of the course assessment structure on the syllabus, for example, you will find this paragraph:

> BUT BUYER BEWARE! You can't wait until the last minute to make this happen! The one way you can screw this up is to keep putting off things until the end of the semester, living under the delusion that you can do a whole bunch of stuff in the last weeks of class to make up for slacking all semester. THIS WON'T WORK! Almost all of these assignments consist of turning in things every week and/or attending scheduled events all semester long . . . AND THERE ARE NO "MAKE-UPS" or "EXTRA CREDIT" or any other additional opportunities offered at the end of the semester to earn points. So choose and plan your semester wisely!!!

On the positive side, as this statement notes, the assessment system for the course eliminates the need for extra credit or make-up exams or penalties for late or missing assignments. If students do not get an assignment in on time, they receive no credit for it; but that's fine, because they still have plenty of other options to earn the same amount of points. And if they come to Boyer looking for extra credit, he responds: "There are hundreds of opportunities for extra credit. It's called the syllabus!" On the negative side, students who miss deadlines throughout the semester may find themselves at the end of the term with not enough options left to pass the course. So this assessment method definitely places a heavier burden of responsibility on students to take control of their own education—and some students will certainly have trouble bearing that responsibility. (We will see how to help students become more effective managers of their learning in Chapter 7.)

During my interview with Boyer in early summer of 2012, he told me that he was planning on introducing a new innovation to the course that fall, one designed to further help students avoid falling too far behind in the course or planning their semester poorly. At the beginning of the next semester, he would be handing to the students a contract that would require them to specify which assignments they would complete. This contract would require them not only to select which assignments would work best for them, but also to map out a semester-long personalized schedule. Boyer was hoping that this innovation to the assessment structure would help students better understand how to budget their time—and their points—over the course of the semester, and would lead to fewer students getting "lost in the sauce."

We saw in the last chapter that strategies for revising your course to foster intrinsic motivation occur along a continuum that might range from wholesale reshaping of your course structure to more modest revisions to your assignments. So, likewise, strategies to orient your course more toward mastery learning can fall on a similar kind of continuum. Boyer, like Kaufman, sits at the far end of that continuum. If you are totally committed to moving a course in the direction of mastery learning, you can use his model as one example of how to de-emphasize specific performances and provide students with a menu of options to demonstrate their learning to you. His model does not exhaust the range of possibilities, though, even at that far end of the continuum. You could just as well offer more choice and control to students by presenting them with three entirely different types of final projects to complete in your course, and letting them choose the one that best reflects the learning they have done. Or you could structure the course in such a way that it covers six broad units, and break down a final examination into six component parts. Students would be told in advance that they would be required to complete only four of those component parts in the final exam, and would be able to select the four that best reflected their interests when they came into the exam room.

But providing students with choice and control can take more modest forms, down to the level of individual assignments. We almost always have the opportunity to offer choice for our students in assignments, or in the mix of assignments we construct. When I teach my British literature survey courses, I do have certain basic themes and works from each literary period that I expect students to have mastered. But I also want them to be able to follow the paths that interest them. So while I might drill them on the works of major authors and themes in our weekly writing exercises, on the midterm I can offer them four essay questions and let them choose three. For the paper assignment I can drop the really specific question I might have formulated about William Wordsworth and give them the opportunity to write about whichever poet has most caught their fancy. (In either case, I have to think creatively about grounding the assignment in their lives in a way that will discourage them from simply parroting someone else's ideas). But whatever choices I make, ultimately I am working to give students the opportunity to carve their own unique path through the course material, rather than forcing them to march through it in lockstep.

All of the strategies described in this chapter, enacted by John Boyer in his World Regions classes, should improve student learning—and more learning should lead to less cheating. At least two experts on cheating, Bernard Whitley and Patricia Keith-Spiegel, make explicit the connection between a mastery learning environment and reduced incentive to cheat. "Using a variety of means of evaluating students' progress," they argue, "makes it more likely that students will encounter forms of evaluation that are more comfortable for them. This comfort level will help reduce performance anxiety and the accompanying motivation for academic dishonesty."[12] Likewise, they claim, "Allowing students the opportunity to be retested on material (using new questions) and redo assignments reduces performance anxiety because students know that if they perform poorly because of illness or other handicapping factors they will have the opportunity to show what they really know."[13]

Note how that word "opportunity" has arisen once again. Many years ago I attended a lecture on teaching by an award-winning political scientist. He spoke about his final exam with an enthusiasm that took me aback: "I look at my final exam as a wonderful opportunity," he said, "for students to show me everything they have learned in that semester." I realized at that moment how differently I thought about my final exams—more like a gauntlet I was throwing down. I still try to remember that political scientist's description of his final exam as I get to the end of each semester, and begin preparing my students for the opportunities they will have to demonstrate their learning to me, rather than for the challenges I will pose to them. Doing so not only helps me describe for the students final exams or projects in ways that might nudge them toward a mastery learning orientation, but it also reminds me that my job is not constructing hurdles; my job is helping other human beings to learn, and the literature on human learning—not to mention the literature on cheating—suggests that I will do so more effectively if I give them more choice and control in the process.

6

LOWERING STAKES

In John Boyer's class, opportunities to earn points on assignments and exams are frequent and plentiful. Even if he did not use a mastery learning assessment system that gave students choices among assignments, the research literature on cheating tells us that merely increasing the frequency of assessments, as he does, should contribute to lower rates of cheating in his course. Remember that in both our historical review and the social science literature, we saw that raising the stakes on an assessment may induce cheating. Infrequent, high-stakes exams—such as the Chinese civil service exams or the kind we saw described in Japanese universities—produce high rates of cheating because they represent the only opportunity for students to earn their grade in the course. The more pressure you put on a single exam, the more likely the chance that students will respond by using any means necessary to succeed on it. The logical inference from this notion would be that the more exams (or quizzes) you give to your students, with lower stakes, the less likely they are to cheat. That might seem immediately counterintuitive to you—the more exams I give to my students, you might be thinking, the more opportunities I am giving them to cheat. You also might be thinking to yourself that the more quizzes or exams you give, the less the students will be learning in the course. After all, every class period they spend taking an exam will be one less exam period devoted to teaching and learning.

That objection rests on the notion, one commonly held by

higher education faculty, that quizzes and exams *measure* learning, while studying and homework and classroom teaching help *produce* learning. That assumption structured my own course design for many years, and led to my having almost no exams in my courses except for the final. Let students write papers to show me what they know, I reasoned; exams just take up valuable class time and are not necessary in my writing or literature courses. In the fall of 2011, however, I first encountered the work of Michelle Miller, a cognitive psychologist from Northern Arizona University who will serve as our guide for this chapter, and who helped me think about tests and exams in a new way. In 2011 Miller published a review in the journal *College Teaching* on recent research in memory and learning theory, and the implications of that research for college and university faculty.[1] After reading this article I was quite abashed to realize, despite many years of reading about teaching and learning, how little I knew about the basic workings of the brain, and the structures that govern memory and learning. I found Miller's explanations so clear and interesting that I ended up profiling her work in a two-part series for the *Chronicle of Higher Education*.[2] She also brought to my attention the work of multiple researchers studying memory and learning theory, and in the months following my interviews with her I dug deeply into their work.

That research helped me understand that the best practices for reducing cheating in our courses coincided with the best practices for increasing learning. So this chapter will begin with a longish introduction of a concept that researchers have dubbed the "testing effect"; once we have become thoroughly acquainted with this important principle of human learning, we will follow Michelle Miller's guidance in thinking about how to implement it in an actual course in order to help your students learn course content more effectively and reduce their incentive to cheat.

Jeffrey K. Karpicke and Henry L. Roediger III, two psychologists who have been working in the field of learning theory for many years now, published an excellent and concise summary of the testing effect in *Science* in February of 2008. Karpicke and Roediger conducted an experiment designed to test the assumption, described above, "that repeated studying promotes learning and that testing represents a neutral event that merely measures learning."[3] In order to check these assumptions, the authors divided their study participants, all college students, into four separate groups. Each group was given forty pairs of English and Swahili words to memorize over the course of a learning period, which included both study time and regular tests to see how many of the word pairs they had memorized (during the tests, they were given the Swahili word and asked to remember its English equivalent). In the first group, the students had the entire word pair list (all forty pairs) to memorize during their study period and were tested on the entire list for all five exams they were given. For the second group, whenever a student had learned one of the word pairs and successfully identified it on a test, it was removed from the student's study list *but remained on all subsequent exams.* So this group was no longer able to study the words in between exams, even though they continued to be tested on them. In the third group any word pairs that were successfully identified on an exam were dropped from subsequent exams *but remained on the study list of words available for them to study;* in the fourth group, successfully identified word pairs were dropped both from the student's study list and from subsequent exams.

The authors conducted all of these study periods and exams

during the first part of the experiment, which they called the "learning phase."[4] By the end of this learning phase, members of all four groups had all forty word pairs memorized; all four groups were able to complete that memorization task at roughly the same rate of speed. But Karpicke and Roediger were especially interested in seeing the effects of their experimental conditions on long-term retention. Consequently they recalled all four groups into the laboratory a week after the learning phase had concluded and gave them one final test on the word pairs. During that intervening week, the students no longer had access to the word pair list, so could no longer study.

The differences in the results of that final test, designed to measure long-term retention, are astonishing. A week after the learning phase, students in the first and second groups were able to recall around 80 percent of the Swahili-English word pairs; students in the third and fourth groups were unable to recall more than around 35 percent of the pairs they had successfully memorized just a week earlier. The differences among the groups now come into sharper focus: in the first and second groups, students were tested on all word pairs on all five exams; in the third and fourth groups, word pairs that students had successfully memorized for an exam were dropped from all subsequent exams. This distinction becomes especially clear when groups two and three are put next to each other. Students in group two, who were tested on all word pairs but did not have access to all word pairs during the study condition, still remembered 80 percent of the word pairs a week later; students who had access to all word pairs during the study condition *but were not tested on all of them* could remember only 35 percent of the word pairs a week later.

The conclusion the authors draw from these results seems inevitable: "testing (and not studying) is the critical factor for promoting long-term recall."[5] This phenomenon has been hanging around in the literature of cognitive psychology for many years now, but a series of new studies by Karpicke and Roediger and others have pushed it to the forefront of the literature on human learning. All of those studies conclude definitively that testing, not studying, seems to provide the most effective way for students to learn course material. Even if that does not seem counterintuitive to you, as it did initially to me, it certainly runs counter to the way many of us operate our courses —especially larger introductory courses, in which we probably test infrequently but admonish students to study as much as possible. Students in such courses, Karpicke and Roediger's experiment would suggest, may well learn the material deeply enough in order to succeed on individual tests they are taking during the course (specific learning phases), but they remember far less of it once they pass out of those specific learning phases and move onto the next unit of the course or the next semester. If you're like me, you certainly hope that students will remember what they learn in your classes beyond the confines of the single semester we spend with them.

This may apply to simple tasks, you may be thinking, such as short lists of English-Swahili word pairs. But does it apply to semester-long courses, often containing complex material? How can we know that the testing effect described by Karpicke and Roediger extends into real college classroom situations?

This was precisely the question addressed in a summary article by Roediger and two colleagues from Washington University in St. Louis, Mark A. McDaniel and Kathleen B. McDermott, published under the apt title of "Generalizing Test-Enhanced Learning from the Laboratory to the Classroom."[6] The article provides an overview of three experimental studies that were designed to move the theory of the testing effect out of the laboratory and into more typical learning conditions for college students. In the first of those studies, the authors had students read short articles from a psychological journal. They then separated the subjects into four groups: one group took a multiple-choice exam on the main concepts in the article, another took a short-answer exam, a third simply studied key concepts from the article, and a fourth had no reinforcement at all. Three days later, the subjects were then recalled to the lab and given a final test, which contained a mix of multiple-choice and short-answer questions. The results of the experiment look exactly as the testing effect would predict: the highest scores on both multiple-choice and short-answer questions came from the groups that took the tests immediately after reading the articles. And here the researchers noted an additional distinction that will become more prominent in the next two studies: the highest scores of all, on both multiple-choice and short-answer exams, came from those students who had initially taken the short-answer exams.

The second experiment simulated a college classroom and testing environment even more accurately. Students were given thirty-minute lectures on art history, followed again by the four possible conditions: no reinforcement, studying key concepts, a multiple-choice exam, or a short-answer exam. But here, in order to better imitate the situation of students who might learn a concept in early September and not take their midterm until mid-October, the researchers postponed the follow-up test for thirty days. "This type of delay," they explain, "simulates the retention interval for a test in college."[7] Once again, the results were consistent with the testing effect, and confirmed the first experiment's conclusion that short-answer tests provided the most effective means of promoting long-term retention. Students who had taken the short-answer tests after the lecture were able to answer close to half of the questions correctly after thirty days; students who had merely studied answered only around 35 percent correctly. (Note that the group which merely studied the concepts afterward still scored much higher than the students who had no reinforcement whatsoever; they clocked in at around 20 percent, which would suggest that study without testing still has some value for our students).

The third and most convincing of their three studies, though, comes when they move out of the laboratory altogether and reproduce these same conditions in a web-based course at the University of New Mexico. There they used a complicated structure across both students and course material in order to recreate the conditions from the laboratory: testing or restudying material presented to students in the course. The experiment spanned six weeks, with three weeks for each of two learning phases followed by a unit test. This experiment allowed all of the conditions that would apply in our courses and students to come into play and potentially disrupt the testing effect; the instructors had no way of influencing how much students studied outside the controlled conditions, or what types of students they were, or what other events may have been taking place in their lives. But even with all of these potentially disruptive factors entering the picture, as they would in any of our college courses, McDaniel, Roediger, and McDermott still found a robust testing effect:

> The patterns shadowed those described . . . for the laboratory experiments. Testing effects were evident, with both short-answer and multiple-choice quizzes augmenting performance on unit examinations relative to when content was not quizzed. Focused reading of the facts, on the other hand, did not boost examination performance. As in the laboratory findings, short-answer quizzing produced significantly higher performance on the unit examinations than did multiple-choice quizzing or focused reading of the target facts.[8]

So in addition to confirming the general testing effect, they also confirmed the finding from the first study on the value of short-answer quizzes or tests as the ones most likely to boost long-term retention.

The authors conclude, as we might expect, that "quizzing benefits learning, and that it does so more than focused reading of target facts."[9] The one question you might still have left to ask at this point would be *why* this would be so. What creates the testing effect? Although the answer to that question begins to take us somewhat far afield, I do want to provide at least a brief explanation, if only to convince you that this is a real phenomenon. Michelle Miller offers an excellent summary of the key principles in learning theory that account for the testing effect in her article on recent research in memory and its implications for our teaching. For much of its young life as a field of study, Miller explains, cognitive theorists used a model of human memory that had been developed in the 1960s. This influential model divided human memory into three stages or parts: sensory perception, short-term memory, and long-term memory. According to the researchers who developed this model, Miller writes, "these three components worked in concert to perform information processing—i.e., turning sensory experience into a 'code' that can be stored and retrieved when needed."[10] You can envision these three parts of the memory system as three distinct boxes: anything we perceive lands in the first box; a much smaller set of all that we perceive lands in the short-term memory box; and an even smaller subset of that material finds its way into the long-term memory box, where it remains available for us to use long after our perception of it has faded.

Despite the powerful hold that this theory once had on the field, Miller continues, "vanishingly few cognitive researchers" —including the scientists who developed this theory—"now believe [this] model to be the best theory of human memory."[11] One major problem with this theory, she says, is that short-term memory turns out to be much more complex than this model posits. And this theory does not do a very good job of explaining why certain information moves from the perceptual field into short-term memory, or how it does so. But whatever other problems this theory contains, the main shift away from it has come from the discovery that our long-term memories can actually store a huge amount of material. A much greater set of what we experience and perceive goes into our long-term memory than researchers previously had posited.

This newly realized storage capacity might seem like a wonderful discovery for those of us who are trying to help other human beings learn—but ultimately it simply shifts the challenges of teaching and learning to a different part of the process. "In long-term-memory," Miller explains, "the limiting factor is not storage capacity, but rather the ability to find what you need when you need it. Long-term memory is rather like having a vast amount of closet space—it is easy to store many items, but it is difficult to retrieve the needed item in a timely fashion."[12] According to earlier theories of memory and cognition, the main challenge faced by a learner was how to get material to pass from short-term memory into long-term memory, where it would be available for future recall. According to these newer theories, all of that material we want to learn may easily be passing into our long-term memory—the challenge for us is getting it back out again when we need it.

The testing effect suggests that this very challenge—retrieving material from our long-term memory—is a skill that we can practice and improve. Every time you take a test or quiz, you are drawing material from your long-term memory. In doing so, you are practicing the cognitive skill that proves the greatest challenge for our memories—and in the act of practicing that retrieval skill, you are getting better at it. On a more scientific level, every time you engage in the retrieval of a specific piece of information, you are opening up and strengthening the neural pathways that lead from that long-term memory to your conscious awareness, and those pathways remain more accessible for you the more often you use them. As Cathy N. Davidson notes in *Now You See It: How the Brain Science of Attention Will Change the Way We Live, Work, and Learn*, a common principle in this area of research (attributed to Donald O. Hebb) is that *"neurons that fire together, wire together."* As Davidson explains the principle, "the more we repeat certain patterns of behavior (that's the firing together), the more those behaviors become rapid, then reflexive, then automatic (that's the wiring)."[13] When you practice memory storage and retrieval, you are helping a specific set of neurons fire together; the more frequently they do so, the more firmly you are wiring them together. You are *not* strengthening those connections in the same way, by contrast, when you are simply sitting and staring at your textbook or your notes, or highlighting key facts and ideas. Those activities, while they may be helpful in some respects, do not strengthen those neural pathways to nearly the same extent.

With that simplified but tidy explanation under our belts,[14] we can now state clearly the implications of all of this for our own teaching: the more quizzes and tests we give to our students, the more we are helping them learn the material we want to teach them. We can broaden this principle by rephrasing it slightly: the more times we test students on their recall of our course material, the more we are helping them learn it. Phrasing it in this way lets in the door other forms of testing recall, such as beginning class by asking students to tell you orally what you covered in the previous class. It would cover Socratic teaching methods, for example, in which you spend class time asking questions of students based on the reading or studying they had done, with the intention of testing their knowledge of course concepts and pushing their thinking in new directions. It might cover other kinds of classroom activities as well, ones that require students to draw from their knowledge to tackle some task or challenge you have set for them. As we shall see from Michelle Miller's course, she takes advantage of the testing effect through multiple pathways like these, not just tests and exams.

But before we turn to her specific class, I want to fend off one final objection you might have about the utility of this principle for your courses, especially upper-level ones. A number of commentators wrote in response to my first column in the *Chronicle of Higher Education* on Miller's work that the cognitive skills involved in memory storage and retrieval form only a part of what we want to help our students obtain or develop. Of course that is true; no doubt we all see our learning objectives as moving beyond memorization and encompassing broader and more difficult skills like writing, critical thinking, creative problem solving, and so on. But it's worth noting, even if you see yourself as teaching those higher-order thinking skills, that our students—like all of us—typically need a strong foundation of knowledge and information in their memories before they can begin using those advanced skills. Many of those who commented on the article also rightly pointed out that the internet has made the storage and retrieval of information a much easier task for all of us—but that doesn't change the fact that we rely on memory all the time in the practice of our discipline and trades, not to mention in everyday life. An emergency-room doctor rushing a patient to surgery, a lawyer brought up short by a surprising piece of testimony in a trial, a sales clerk responding to an unexpected question by a customer—in all of those moments, the professional in question has to draw quickly from a memorized store of previous experiences and information. Certainly the ability to apply the information from memory to a new situation and respond accordingly represents a different and more complex thinking skill—but people can't get to that more complex skill without access to their medical, legal, or professional knowledge.

Those of us in higher education surely know that from our own experiences. When a student in my survey course on British literature asks me about the Irish potato famine, she should expect me to expound upon the role that the British government played in exacerbating that "natural" disaster, but she should also expect me to know—without my having to stop class and Google it—that the first potato crop failed in 1845, and that crop failures continued for the next half-dozen years. Likewise, if I expect my students to understand the complex historical and literary relationship between Ireland and England, I want them to know roughly where the famine falls in the historical timeline of that relationship. I might not care whether they know the exact years of the worst crop failures, but I do care that they know how the crisis related to the rise of industrialism and economic theory in the nineteenth century, how it influenced the writings of Marx and Engels, and how it precipitated an Irish diaspora. To understand those more complex historical issues, students must know the approximate dates of the famine. So memory matters, even for those of us teaching the most complex cognitive skills we can imagine. And if memory matters, then we should provide our students with the best possible help in committing our course material to memory, and having the foundational tools they need to pursue higher-level thinking tasks.

Michelle Miller gives her students that help in multiple ways in her Cognitive Psychology course at Northern Arizona University. She described the course to me as a "core requirement for psychology majors that typically enrolls 70–80 sophomore students"—just the kind of large introductory course, she noted, in which cheating would be a very likely possibility.[15] And just the kind of large introductory course, I would add, in which an instructor might be tempted to manage her time commitments by falling back on infrequent, traditional forms of assessment: a few multiple-choice exams along the way, a final, and maybe a research paper. I wouldn't bat an eye at seeing a faculty member use such an assessment plan in a core course that enrolled between seventy and eighty students.

And indeed, you will find two multiple-choice exams in Miller's course, along with a multiple-choice final exam. But as you might expect from a teacher who was a 2011 appointee to the ranks of Northern Arizona University's Distinguished Teaching Fellows, Miller fills out her assessment structure with a much wider array of methods designed to help her students practice the retrieval of key course concepts *and* put them into practice both in and out of the classroom. First and most obviously, Miller makes use of weekly online multiple-choice quizzes to ensure that students are keeping up with the reading. These quizzes are taken by the students outside of class and are open book. Students are allowed to take each quiz twice and retain only the highest of their two scores—another example of the kind of mastery learning exercise that we saw in John Boyer's class. Miller believes that these quizzes have made a substantive impact: as she said to me in an interview about the course, "I suspect that the reading quizzes make a meaningful difference in learning and grades; my exam scores are similar to what they were semesters ago when the course was an upper-division elective with mostly seniors using the same book." Multiple-choice quizzes like these are an easily applied assessment structure in just about any course, and the ability to offer them online can help allay possible concerns about "giving up" too much class time for additional assessments or about giving up too much of *your* time for evaluating them.

There are two specific aspects of these quizzes that are essential to note, however. First, the students do *not* receive the answers to the quiz questions as soon as they have taken them—a practice that you see, for example, in many online tutorials. As Miller explains to the students on the syllabus, they are welcome to ask her about the correct answers to any quiz question they are uncertain about, but they have to take the initiative to do that. The merits of handling online quizzes this way can be easily seen by considering a cheating scandal that was reported in the *Chronicle of Higher Education* in June of 2012. A group of students in an online course learned how to cheat on a quiz system that resembled Miller's except for the fact that the students received immediate feedback on each answer they gave, so they could see whether they had answered the question correctly. As a student explained to a *Chronicle* reporter:

> If he and his friends got together to take the test jointly, they could paste the questions they saw into [a] shared Google Doc, along with the right or wrong answers. The schemers would go through the test quickly, one at a time, logging their work as they went. The first student often did poorly, since he had never seen the material before, though he would search an online version of the textbook on Google Books for relevant keywords to make informed guesses. The next student did significantly better, thanks to the cheat sheet, and subsequent test-takers upped their scores even further. They took turns going first.[16]

For learning purposes, in an ideal world, it probably makes more sense to have students receive immediate feedback on their answers after they have given them. If you want to reduce opportunities for cheating, though, Miller's plan might be the better one. After all, she can give students in the course feedback on their answers when they request it, and she can review the material from the quizzes during class time, so the students still can and will receive some feedback within a short time of taking the online quiz.

Another essential aspect of Miller's structure is that the online quizzes and major exams are in the same format, multiple choice. We saw from Karpicke and Roediger's experiments that short-answer testing may produce better learning than any other format. But when you are teaching courses of over seventy students, you can imagine how the time commitment required to give and grade short-answer quizzes or tests starts to rise exponentially. So multiple-choice testing may represent the most feasible option for teachers under those conditions, one that still allows them to take advantage of the testing effect. But an important caveat needs to be established here. Research on human learning suggests that one area that seems to be more complex than instructors might imagine is *transfer*. This concept refers to the ability of a learner to take knowledge or a skill developed in one context and apply it in a different one—so, for example, to take knowledge that they have practiced applying in a multiple-choice exam and be able to transfer it to a short-answer exam. According to multiple studies cited by Susan Ambrose and her colleagues in *How Learning Works*, "transfer occurs neither often nor automatically, and . . . the more dissimilar the learning and transfer contexts, the less likely successful transfer will occur."[17] So if you spend the entire semester giving your students multiple-choice quizzes and then give them a long essay as a final exam, you are expecting students to make a transfer that they likely find far more difficult than you realize.[18]

The end result of this notion is that, whatever type of assessment we give to our students on our major exams and assignments, we need to give them *prior* practice in developing those skills or applying that knowledge in that specific context. So if you are going to give your students multiple-choice final exams, they should be taking multiple-choice quizzes along the way. If you are going to be giving students essay final exams, they should be taking weekly essay quizzes. If you have both types of assessment on your final exam, let them practice both. Any type of quiz or exam has the potential to help students deepen their learning through the testing effect; but what we know about transfer helps us understand that we have to help students practice the skills or apply the knowledge we want them to demonstrate to us on our major exams. None of this means, by the way, that students are not capable of transferring knowledge from one domain to another, or from one assessment type to another, and that you should therefore limit your assessments to one single type throughout the entire semester. Students can learn to apply skills or demonstrate knowledge in multiple formats and contexts, and the more of those you offer, the more likely they are to retain the material. But whatever you ultimately expect of them on your major assessments, you should first allow them to practice on lower-stakes, more frequent assessments— just as Miller does with her online multiple-choice quizzes, designed to prepare students for the final exam.

Like every good teacher, Miller wants her students to see the relevance of her course and her discipline to the world outside of her classroom. So in addition to the quizzes and the exams, Miller's students complete two other kinds of graded assignments. She uses a web-based system called Coglab, which requires students to participate in simulated research experiments in psychology. Doing so allows them to gain a first-hand understanding of the experience of designing and participating in real psychology experiments. Near the end of the semester, they are responsible for a project in which they create a "realistic, practical solution to a problem or question" based on the work they have been doing in the course. These "Application Projects," as she calls them, are excellent examples of the kind of grounded assessments we reviewed in Chapter 4—we can hear in the title phrase, in fact, echoes of Andy Kaufman's student discussing the notion of "applied" courses. So, for example, one semester Miller gave the students the assignment to "draft a memo to the university student council explaining why they should not spend $10,000 on memory enhancing software based on some sketchy scientific claims." The students had to reference an empirical research article she gave them, but were otherwise encouraged to "get creative with it," as she put it. "Draft a speech to give to the local school board," runs another project assignment, this time echoing Sarah Cavanagh's presentations to the local middle school students, "explaining the advantages of bilingualism."

In both Coglab and these application projects, students have to ground the concepts and information they are learning for the quizzes and exams in other environments, whether those be the labs of working psychologists or the field of memory research. We learned already about the difficulties that learners have with transferring what they have learned to new contexts, and that we cannot simply expect such transfer to happen automatically. So if students are going to be evaluated on their ability to apply concepts and information outside of the lab, then they should have some opportunities to practice this skill in advance of those graded assignments. Miller gives them just such practice with her in-class activities: brief, low-stakes exercises that ask students to—in the words of the syllabus—"discuss, reflect on, or apply material we are working on that day." So, for example, she might pause in the middle or at the end of class and ask students to write a short response to the following question: "Describe one everyday example of the impact of cues on retrieval from long-term memory." Or: "When are you best off relying on intuition . . . and when should you ignore intuition?" It might seem overwhelming to imagine a faculty member responding to short-answer questions like these every day in a class of seventy or more students. Miller does not typically write detailed responses to each student, however. She explains on the syllabus that students will receive full credit for "good-faith effort"; she told me that she "might pull a few to comment on in class, or make a few written comments if the student is way off base," but otherwise simply gives credit for a reasonable response of any kind. This seems especially appropriate given the low stakes of these assessments; although she has at least one of them during almost every class period—which, as she pointed out to me, helps ensure better attendance in a large course— they account for a total of only 10 percent of the student's final grade.

These in-class activities strike me as accomplishing two important objectives. First, they provide opportunities for students to think about application of the course concepts outside of the classroom, thus helping prepare them for the Coglab experiments and the application project. In giving students such advance preparation, Miller is reducing the number of students who might approach those assignments with anxiety and uncertainty, and might resort to cheating as a consequence. But more important, the in-class activities represent another way in which Miller can take advantage of the memory retrieval practice that we learned about from research on the testing effect. Remember that the principle underlying the testing effect is that students benefit from frequent retrieval and rehearsal of the concepts and information they are learning. We might most easily imagine quizzes and tests as the primary means by which students engage in such retrieval and rehearsal, but those are not the only means available to them or us. Students can practice retrieval and rehearsal activities while they are studying, for example, by studying with the book closed. Instead of simply rereading their textbook or notes over and over again, in other words, they can close their books and practice retrieving the main ideas from their notes or the chapter by talking about them with one another or by reproducing them in different forms on a new notebook page: as an outline, or in paragraph form, or even as a concept map. That kind of studying will prove much more effective than the typical studying behavior of most college students. (We will consider this in more detail in the next chapter.)

And so, likewise, Michelle Miller helps students begin the process of practicing retrieval and rehearsal of course information with her in-class activities. Consider again the first example I gave of a question she might pose to students as an in-class activity: "Describe one everyday example of the impact of cues on retrieval from long-term memory." Envision such a question being posed to students after they had read material on the notion of "cues" and heard a brief lecture on the topic. Students are then asked to close their books and respond to that question in writing. Doing so requires two intellectual activities. First, students have to remember and rehearse what they have just learned. All of the in-class activities, Miller explained to me, are like this one in that they "require students to access the material from memory in order to come up with a reasonably thoughtful response." Second, they ask students to begin building their own connections between the course material and the world outside of the classroom. "I tend to emphasize," she told me, "application to everyday life or other opportunities for students to personalize the material." That emphasis first helps students prepare for the application they will be doing on their out-of-class project. But giving students the opportunity to personalize the material also helps them create richer connections between what they are learning and what they already know, which can help students—as it can help all of us—remember ideas and information more deeply.

Miller's in-class activities do not always take the form of short writing exercises like this one. Sometimes, for example, the students are given the opportunity to discuss the question in small groups and then turn in a group response. "The critical point," she says, "is to get students actively responding during class, regardless of the exact specifics of the activity." And we can envision easily enough that, in some cases, the written component might not even be necessary to take advantage of the benefits of frequent retrieval and rehearsal. Oftentimes we conclude lectures or mini-lectures in class by asking students if they have any questions in response to what we have just presented. If you're like me, you have plenty of experience in hearing nothing but crickets chirping in response to that question. A much better way to conclude a lecture, according to what we have covered in this chapter, would be to ask students to close their notebooks, and then to spend ten minutes posing specific questions designed to elicit students' recall of what they have just heard. I know that sometimes instructors shy away from this kind of activity, not wanting to appear like a drill sergeant grilling the recruits. But attitude and tone can make a huge difference when you are engaging students in the classroom; you could conduct such an exercise like a drill sergeant, but you could also conduct it like a researcher inviting a colleague into a fascinating conversation. You can also remove some of the tension from the room if you make it clear, on the syllabus and from the first day of the semester, that all lectures will conclude with the opportunity for students to test what they have learned with some oral questions and answers in class. Make it clear that you are doing so because this quizzing will help them learn by allowing them to practice retrieval and rehearsal—not because you want to embarrass anyone or catch anyone who has been napping during the lecture.

None of the testing-effect strategies I have been describing in the work of Michelle Miller—frequent online quizzes and regular in-class activities that require retrieval and rehearsal—are revolutionary ones. As she acknowledged to me during our interview, the in-class activities are partially modeled on the now-famous low-stakes assessment model of the "minute paper," in which a teacher concludes a lecture by asking students to write down one key concept that they learned during the class period. The minute paper has a thousand variations, and Miller's in-class activities could be seen as a series of such variations. It's also time to acknowledge that constructing a course using these activities cannot guarantee that you will not have cheating—just as none of the strategies that I am covering in the four chapters of Part II will guarantee that. But if we keep in mind the foundational principle of the book, that the best means we have to reduce cheating is to increase motivation and learning, than I think we can take two essential points away from Michelle Miller's research on memory and learning, as well as from the ways in which she applies that research to her own course.

First, provide frequent opportunities for students to practice retrieval and rehearsal of the information that you want them to learn. That process can start from the very class period in which you present them with the information, in the ways in which you pose questions and problems to students in class; it can continue outside of class with online exercises or quizzes; and it can be solidified in the form of the tests you give. Each time your students are able to recall your course material from memory, according to the experiments of cognitive psychologists like Karpicke and Roediger, they are sealing up neural connections that will help them recall that material more easily the next time, and that will lead to greater long-term learning. Of course we have not by any means exhausted the possible ways in which a college faculty member can give students practice with retrieval and rehearsal; the important point here is not to faithfully reproduce Michelle Miller's example in detail, but to understand the principle of the testing effect and see how you can apply it in your classes. I have used short-answer writing exercises in my literature courses for many years now, at the beginning of almost every class, and I have seen the great potential for taking advantage of the testing effect—but it was not until I learned about the testing effect myself that I understood their power, and began planning them more carefully in order to reinforce student learning of the key concepts in the course. I suspect that many faculty will already have course features that give students the opportunity to practice retrieval and rehearsal and may, like me, now have the opportunity to think a little bit more deliberately about how you deploy them in your courses.

Second, faculty should provide at least some of those opportunities for retrieval and rehearsal in low-stakes formats, and particularly in the formats on which students will have to engage in their high-stakes assignments or exams. The difficulty that students—and perhaps all learners—have in transferring knowledge or skills from one context to another means that if we want them to succeed on our high-stakes evaluations, we should give them plenty of opportunities to practice their skills on similarly formatted low-stakes assessments. If your students take a high-stakes final exam in multiple-choice format, you should have them taking lower-stakes multiple-choice quizzes throughout the semester. If your students take a high-stakes final essay exam, have them respond to essay questions in class throughout the semester. Ideally, you are testing students in more than one format, and asking them to do at least some writing, but with the course sizes that many of us have to manage these days, that can be difficult. While the research does seem to suggest that longer-term learning happens when students are writing, as opposed to taking multiple-choice exams, the differences between the two were not overly large ones. The format matters less than the alignment between the low- and high-stakes assessments, and the frequency of opportunities you give to students.

We began this chapter with what might have seemed to you a counterintuitive notion: that the more assessments you give to your students, the less cheating you will have. I suspect that most faculty who have taught for a while will have had some version of the following experience, at least if you ever teach classes that allow for student discussion. You pose a question about the reading to your class, and a student formulates an interesting response to the question, one that reflects his reading of the material but puts his own specific spin on it. Later that week, the student comes back to the same idea in a short-answer response on the midterm exam. Still later in that semester, the student takes the idea a little further and uses it as the starting point for a major essay for the course. The first time the student spoke that idea aloud in class, it created a new connection for him. During the exam, the idea was more easily recalled in written form because it had been discussed in class. The idea continued to hang around in the student's head, ultimately forming the basis for further research and understanding in the essay the student prepared. The research on cognitive theory that we have covered in this chapter tells us that this student may remember that idea longer and more fully than anything else he learned in the course. The more opportunities we give to students to rehearse what they have learned in these ways, the less likely they will be to seek easy answers, outside the confines of academic honesty, for what they need to succeed in your course.

7

INSTILLING SELF-EFFICACY

As the father of five children, I frequently get roped into serving as the coach or assistant coach on youth sports teams. Despite the fact that I stopped playing all sports except golf and ping pong (do those count?) in my freshman year of high school, I have now imparted my sports-oriented wisdom to young people in the areas of baseball, football, and soccer over the past dozen years or so. As a result, I have become thoroughly familiar with what I call the "good jobbing" of American youth today, and in fact am one of the main practitioners of this dubious coaching technique. No matter what a kid on one of my teams does, I find myself saying "Good job!" to it. Hit a single in baseball? "Good job!" Scored a soccer goal? "Good job!" When the child has actually *not* done a good job, I add some clarification. Dropped a pass in football? "Good job! You really dove well for that ball!" Struck out at the plate? "Good job! Way to swing at that pitch, instead of watching a called third strike!" I can find a reason and language to praise almost anything a child does in a sporting event, as long as they are not sitting in the field picking dandelions in the middle of the game. (Although I am tempted sometimes to congratulate those children on engaging in civil disobedience with their passive protests against the madness that youth sports can sometimes become.) I am quite adept at the skill of "good jobbing," which is probably why I am in such demand as a coach.

The first technique that might occur to you when you are thinking about helping students overcome self-efficacy prob-

lems, which ranked fourth in our list of factors that might induce students to cheat, is to engage in lots of "good jobbing" in
your classroom. But there is a problem with this—one that occurs on a smaller level in children's sports, but becomes much
more intense in higher education. If we do nothing but praise
children for their efforts, we give them a false sense of their skill
level. This really doesn't matter much to five-year-olds on a soccer field. Over the course of the next few years, they will gradually be able to see for themselves how they stack up with their
peers on the soccer pitch, and no amount of "good jobbing"
will cover up the significant and visible differences that begin to
emerge between excellent and poor athletes as the children enter middle and high school. But it can create a significant problem for college students, in that poorly gauged *overconfidence* in
their knowledge of course material can lead them to *under-
study*—and hence might be as likely to induce cheating as a lack
of confidence in their abilities.

To help instill a strong but realistic sense of self-efficacy in our
students, one that will give them the confidence they need to
undertake the challenges we give to them without underesti-
mating the effort it will take, we can look to two very concrete
strategies: improving *student metacognition*, and improving *faculty communication*. I will take them up in that order, because I
believe that improving student metacognition requires harder
thinking about your teaching, and has the potential to inspire
deeper changes in the way that you conduct your classes. Once
you have made your decision about how—or whether—to make
those changes, you can then build more effective communication into just about any course with the strategies I will cover in
the final part of the chapter.

I was first introduced to the fancy five-cent notion of metacognition by Stephen Chew, a cognitive psychologist who has pro-

duced a terrific series of YouTube videos for college and university students on how they can learn to study more effectively. When I first discovered these videos, I wrote a profile of Chew and the videos for a *Chronicle of Higher Education* column. I focused especially on the first video in the series, in which he introduces students to the concept of metacognition.[1] Stephen Chew will serve as our guide through this concept and what it means for our students, and his work in the videos and in the interviews I conducted with him stands behind this entire chapter. But Stephen will join us formally only for a few pages, and then I want to introduce you to a group of physicists at MIT who published an essay about how they reduced cheating in their large, introductory physics courses—and did so, at least in my analysis, by giving their students a significant metacognitive boost.

Put as simply as possible, according to Chew, metacognition "is a person's awareness of his or her own level of knowledge and thought processes. In education, it has to do with students' awareness of their actual level of understanding of a topic."[2] Students with excellent metacognitive skills have a clear and accurate picture of how well they know the material they are studying; those with poor metacognitive skills have an inaccurate picture of their learning. Although a small number of students may underestimate their knowledge about the material they are trying to learn (which could result in low self-efficacy), more typically students err in the other direction. Students with poor metacognition, Chew says, are usually "grossly overconfident in their level of understanding. They think they have a good understanding when they really have a shallow, fragmented understanding that is composed of both accurate information and misconceptions."[3] If you have ever had a distraught student visit your office hours after an exam, lamenting that he thought he knew the material cold and then bombed an exam, you were likely staring at a student with poor metacognitive skills.

The reason that those poor metacognitive skills cause problems for students is that they lead them to make poor study decisions, which then have consequences for their performances on exams or assignments. As Chew puts it, "once students feel they have mastered material, they will stop studying, usually before they have the depth and breadth of understanding they need to do well. On exams, they will often believe their answers are absolutely correct, only to be shocked when they make a bad grade."[4] So a student with poor metacognitive skills may imagine that two hours of studying for a major exam has given him complete mastery of the material; a student with excellent metacognitive skills recognizes that two hours of studying has only scratched the surface of what she needs for such an important exam, and will continue working for another six or eight hours. The student with poor metacognitive skills will not realize the depth of his error in judgment, though, until he is sitting in front of the exam and realizing how badly he has miscalculated—or, for those students with especially poor metacognitive skills, until you give them back their failed exam.

In the interview I conducted with Chew, I asked him about the single best strategy that faculty could use in order to help their students improve their metacognitive skills. "The best way to reduce the impact of poor metacognition," Chew said, "is to use formative assessment during teaching. Formative assessments are brief, low-stakes activities that students do in order to give both themselves and the teacher feedback about their level of understanding. There is a wide assortment of assessments that faculty can use, such as think-pair-share activities, minute papers, and so-called 'clicker' questions."[5] I noted in the last chapter that Michelle Miller's in-class activities represent a form of the "minute paper," and we can now put those activities in the terms described by Chew here as "formative assessments." The more such opportunities that the students have to test out their knowledge and receive feedback on it in formative assessments like the ones Chew mentioned, the more accurate a picture they will have of their own learning—and the more accurate that picture is, the more they will be able to make good decisions about their studying. The better those study decisions are, the less likely they will be to find themselves stuck behind the eight-ball in the hours before an exam, or in the final weeks of the semester, knowing that their only option for success in the course is an academically dishonest one.

The most effective low-stakes assessments you can give, of course—as we have already reviewed in our chapter on the testing effect—are ones that will reappear in high-stakes form on your exams or assignments. So whatever skills the students will need to succeed on your high-stakes assessments, they should have had multiple opportunities to practice and receive feedback on those skills on prior low-stakes assessments. Doing so will both help them learn the course material more deeply through the testing effect, and will help them gain a clearer picture of their own learning (that is, better metacognition). (And, as a helpful bonus, it will help you gain a clearer picture of what students are learning or not learning in your class, allowing you to modify your teaching accordingly.)

In his class, Chew uses "clickers" in order to provide the students with a better understanding of their knowledge in the course, and to give them practice on the kinds of questions that they will see on the exam:

> I present the class with a multiple-choice question similar to ones
> that will be on the exam. Students select their answers individu-
> ally, and I poll the class. They can then discuss their answer with

other students, after which I poll the class again. Finally, we discuss the answers as a class. This gives me a sense of how well students understand the material. I can identify and address problem areas. I also emphasize that the question I use is similar in difficulty level to questions they will see on exams, so if they did not answer correctly or were confused, they need to improve their understanding. Formative assessment helps students study and learn more effectively *before* exams, and they are less likely to feel "tricked" by questions they didn't expect. The actual exam should never be the first time the faculty or the students get feedback about the actual level of student understanding.[6]

Done well, the kind of formative assessment that Chew describes here can help address both ends of the metacognitive spectrum. Students who overestimate their understanding of the topic should see their mistake if they are consistently getting the answers to the questions wrong, or are having to guess at the answers. Students who are underconfident in their learning—and hence have the kind of low self-efficacy that might lead to cheating—should be able to gain confidence by consistently doing well on the clicker questions, especially if they know that those same types of questions will appear on their graded exams.[7] In neither case, as Chew points out, will students feel "tricked" by what they see on an exam, or even anticipate feeling "tricked" by an exam. And as you may remember, one aspect of self-efficacy that made a difference in cheating was whether or not the students felt they would be assessed fairly by their professors. The formative assessments described by Chew give students a very clear picture of how they will be evaluated, reducing any potential feelings they might have of receiving unfair treatment on their exams.

But you don't need clickers to create formative assessments in your class, as we saw with the example of Michelle Miller; you can use such assessments in a variety of ways, and you can even attach points to them if you prefer, though you want to keep those stakes as low as possible. To offer another example, suppose that you typically give your students a midterm and a final exam that require them to synthesize concepts or information from your course in several long essay questions. How can you prepare your students to do well on those exams, improve their metacognition, and reduce their incentive to cheat? The additional paper assignments you have for the course won't help, nor will the presentation you also assign. In those cases you are asking the students to do something different, drawing on different skill sets. To help them develop the skills they will need to succeed on your essay exams, you might occasionally ask them to perform concept syntheses in class in ten- or fifteen-minute writing exercises throughout the semester. Once a week, for example, you might begin class by asking your students to write a two-paragraph response to just such a synthesis question. Each of those responses might count for a very small fraction of their final grade. Imagine the difference between a student who has spent the semester gamely reviewing her notes every once in a while and believing that she has the concepts mastered, but who has never attempted a written synthesis of those concepts, and a student who has had a dozen opportunities to practice writing a synthesis and has received feedback on how he has done. Which student will have learned this skill more deeply and effectively? Which student will be less likely to bomb the midterm, become terrified about the final exam, and be motivated to do whatever it takes—honest or otherwise—in order to ace that final exam?

Practicing with short writing exercises to prepare students for essay exams will work only in some disciplines, obviously, so you will have to translate this example into whatever discipline in which you are teaching. The principle is simple enough: take a look at whatever you require of students on your high-stakes assessments, and break it down into smaller chunks or pieces on which you can give students low-stakes assessments during the intervals between those higher-stakes exams or assignments. Doing so will not only make use of the testing effect in order to reinforce your course content in your student's brains, but it will also help firm up their metacognitive awareness of their knowledge in your course. And doing both of these things will reduce the incentive for students to cheat. To hearken back to the first historical situation we considered, the ancient Olympics, imagine you were the world's fastest sprinter, and you *knew* you were faster than everyone else—why in the world would you bother bribing the judges in order to ensure your victory? The students' knowledge, and their metacognitive awareness of that knowledge, can be one of the best remedies we have against cheating.

The clicker strategy described by Stephen Chew was initially developed by Eric Mazur, a physicist at Harvard University. To help see more clearly how frequent low-stakes assessment activities can both improve metacognitive skills and reduce cheating, I want to turn to a group of four physicists across town from Mazur, at MIT, who published an essay in the January 2010 edition of the online journal *Physics Education Research* about how they reduced cheating on homework assignments and increased learning and course retention in their large, introductory physics courses for nonmajors.[8] Their study focused initially on two large sections of the courses in the fall of 2003. With approximately 215 students in each of those two sections, the courses were taught in traditional lecture-recitation format: the faculty offered three lectures per week, as well as two recitation sessions. Attendance was not required at either the lecture or recitation sessions; unsurprisingly, attendance rates clocked in at a rather low 60 percent. The major assessments for the course, following an initial pretest to check students' knowledge prior to taking the course, included three in-class examinations and a final exam. But students also had to complete weekly homework assignments: one of them an electronic problem that they solved through an online homework system called MasteringPhysics (worth 10 percent of their total grade in the course), and one of them a written assignment. The physics professors who co-authored the study were concerned about two issues: how much cheating was taking place on those electronic homework assignments, and how many students were either dropping out or doing poorly in the course. They wanted, in part, to understand whether there was a correlation between these two factors—but mostly they wanted to reduce the rates of both cheating and poor performances in the course.

In order to determine how much copying was taking place on the homework assignments, they decided to analyze the amount of time it took students to complete the online homework problems. They estimated that students who were actively and authentically engaged with the homework took ten minutes or more to complete each problem. When they looked at the reports, which indicated how many minutes had elapsed between the time the student opened the problem on a browser and the time it took him to complete the problem, they saw a significant number of students were doing so in a minute or less—less time than it would take to read the problem in its entirety and type in a response, much less actually think about it and work out the answer. Using this time-to-completion factor as their main piece of evidence, they estimated that around 10 percent of the total problems completed in the course had been copied from another source. That gross number of total problems copied breaks down in two important ways. First, the researchers were able to see the number of students who engaged in different rates of copying. They found a small number of students (10 percent) who copied at least half of their homework problems; a majority of students (51 percent) who copied either not at all or less than 10 percent of the problems; and a messier group of "light" or "moderate" copiers (39 percent) who copied between 10 and 50 percent of the problems. Second, and more interestingly—if perhaps still unsurprisingly—they were able to determine that copying intensified as the deadline for the homework approached, and spiked right around deadline time and slightly afterward. Looking more closely at this, they discovered a primary difference between heavy copiers and those who copied little or not at all. The noncopying group, they reported, "does their work in a timely fashion; working steadily over three days before due time and completing ~½ of their problems two days before they are due"; the heavy copy group "typically does only ~10% of their work two days early, and leave[s] almost 60% of the assignment to the final six hours, and about 15% until after it is due." The more work they left until the hours before the deadline, in other words, the more the students were likely to copy.[9]

How does that information square with what we have already learned about cheating? Just as we saw in our opening chapter, we have a small number of students (10 percent) who are cheating regularly, a larger number of students who cheat much less regularly, and a much larger number of students who either do not cheat at all or do so very infrequently. So in that respect what we see in this course matches the basic picture we have of how many of our students engage in academically dishonest behavior. As for the issue of the copying increasing dramatically in the hours before the due date, we can certainly attribute some of that to poor time management on the part of the students—a common enough problem that, as faculty, we have limited ability to help our students overcome. But I think we can also attribute much of this deadline copying to poor metacognition on the students' part. Metacognition in this case would involve a recognition of the difficulty of the homework problems and an assessment of their ability to solve the problems in the required time period. Students with sharp metacognitive skills were obviously aware that these were difficult problems that would challenge their understanding, and so began working on them three days in advance, completing over half of them two days before the due date. Students with poor metacognitive skills, by contrast, assumed that they would be able to complete most of the problems within six hours of the due date and time, and so unwisely left most of them until the day they were due. When faced with the realization that they had badly miscalculated the amount of time they needed to complete the problem, many of them resorted to copying.

And many of them, as a result, did increasingly poorly in the course. The authors looked at the student scores on all five exams, from the pretest to the final, and compared them with the amount of copying that the students did. In simplest terms, they explain, "repeated homework copying" correlates sharply with "severely declining performance relative to class average over the five primary assessments."[10] In other words, the test scores of the heaviest copiers show a mostly steady decline from the beginning of the semester to the final exam. The authors are able to demonstrate that repeated copiers and noncopiers scored in roughly the same range on the pretest. In other words, all students began the course with the same basic set of skills and background knowledge. But as the semester progressed, the students who engaged in repeated copying saw their scores gradually decline from test to test in comparison with noncopiers, culminating in a "copying" final exam score average that was two full standard deviations below the "noncopying" exam score average. The authors make the excellent point, as a result of comparing these averages on the pretest and final exam, that "contrary to the typical belief of American students that innate ability . . . is the principal determiner of exam success, doing all assigned work is a surer route to exam success than innate physics ability."[11] As I see it reflected in this sentence, and in other parts of the article, the authors of this study struck me as driven by the admirable desire to address cheating in their course because cheating reduces learning. They wanted as many students as possible to learn physics, and so they wanted as few students as possible to copy the homework problems.

To achieve these goals, the authors revamped the course entirely, shifting it to what they call a "studio model" following the fall of 2003. They continued to tweak the structure of the course through the fall of 2006, the last semester included in their analysis. (In the first year of trying out the new format, students had the option of signing up for the studio model course or the traditional lecture course; by 2006, all sections of the course had shifted to the studio model.) The changes made to shift the course to a studio model included the following:

> The course was divided into sections of ~75 students each; each section met for 5 h[ours] total each week with one professor and several teaching assistants. During class periods, students were given minilectures interspersed with questions answered using a personal response system followed by peer instruction, hands-on experiments, and group problem-solving sessions, often at the board. Students were broken into groups of not more than 3 and each student group had access to a computer used to enhance demonstrations and collect their experimental data.[12]

They shifted the nature of the homework slightly as well, moving to two assignments per week from MasteringPhysics and one written homework assignment (more frequent assessments, in other words).

The shift to the studio model helped the authors achieve both of the consequences they desired. The total number of problems copied fell from around 11 percent in the fall of 2003 to around 3 percent in the fall of 2006. The fall of 2006, the year of the lowest cheating rate seen in the study, had also included a technical shift the authors made to the MasteringPhysics problems, which made it more difficult for students to copy their answers. But even in 2004 and 2005, when they were still using the previous types of questions, the copy rate dropped by nearly half. The number of students who earned D's or F's in the course dropped by an equally dramatic rate from the fall of 2003 to the spring of 2006. Out of 428 students who began the course in the fall of 2003, 38 of them ultimately failed; out of 619 students who took the studio model courses in the spring of 2006, only 10 of them failed. In their laconic and cautious scientific language, the authors state that "[w]e suspect that reduction in homework copying is responsible for a significant part of this reduction in failure rate."[13] In this quote we arrive once again at the happy juncture that animates Part II of this book, in which we see that the strategies which reduce cheating are precisely the strategies that increase learning. Reducing the amount of students who are copying their homework increases the number of students who are passing the course. I would argue that improved metacognition stands at the heart of this junction, even though the authors of the study do not specifically address that concept. It seems clear enough to me that when students are completing the homework assignments in class, under the guidance of their professors, they are—in addition to gaining more practice at the skills they will need on the exams—receiving a much clearer picture of their ability to *do physics.* That more accurate picture should help them direct their studying and practice more effectively, and make better decisions about how much time and effort they need to commit to the course.

In the second decade of the twenty-first century, a new set of phrases has emerged for describing the phenomenon of professors restructuring their classes in the way described by these physics teachers, from traditional lecture models to ones in which students are actively engaged in problem solving or other course-related work: the "flipped" or "inverted" classroom. The basic idea captured by these phrases (and others like them) is that instead of students sitting passively for lectures on the information or concepts they need to know and then going home to try and apply those concepts or information to answer questions or solve problems, the instructor flips or inverts these elements of the course: students get the basic information they need prior to coming to class and then spend class time working on problems or answering questions with the instructor on hand to guide and supervise. In order to get that information to students beforehand, faculty can videotape their lectures, post presentations to a course website, or provide necessary readings. The students study that material in advance of class, and come to class prepared to work instead of simply to listen. This represents an inversion or flipping of the typical lecture-recitation model of science, technology, engineering, and mathematics courses (usually referred to with the acronym STEM), in which instructors might lecture on key concepts or even model problem-solving techniques in class and then expect students to go home and solve homework problems on their own.[14] That is not exactly what was happening in those MIT physics courses in the fall of 2003, since the instructors still presented key concepts to the students during class time through "minilectures," as they describe them. In a truly flipped classroom, those minilectures would be presented to the students prior to their coming to class, either in videotaped format or through written materials. When these physics instructors shifted to a studio model, though, and had students working on practice problems in class, they were employing at least one of the main strategies of the flipped classroom—having students spend time in class practicing their problem-solving skills and receiving directed feedback from the instructor. And it's that feature of the flipped classroom, I would argue—low-stakes classroom activities with direct feedback from the instructor—that helps students improve their metacognitive skills in the course.

As has been suggested by Derek Bruff, Director of the Center for Teaching Excellence at Vanderbilt University, none of this may seem very revolutionary to humanities or qualitatively oriented social science faculty. In these fields, professors typically assign reading in advance of the day's lecture or discussion and expect students to come prepared to engage in discussions or other interactive activities.[15] But speaking as a humanities professor and drawing upon many conversations I have had with my colleagues on and off campus, as well as observations I have done in their classrooms, I can point out one major problem with assuming that my co-disciplinary colleagues have nothing to learn from the flipped classroom and the improved metacognition it can bring to our students—namely, that in my discipline and many others, students often do not do the reading. During the years I directed the Honors Program at my college, I had an office right next to a lounge area where students congregated and socialized between classes. I was astounded at how many times I heard our best students on campus discussing reading assignments they had skimmed, skipped, or forgotten about. It scared me to think about how many non-Honors students were following their lead. But of course we don't give students much reason to do the reading in advance of class if we step to the front of the room on most days and deliver lectures about the readings we have assigned. In that case, I would have complete sympathy with students who don't bother to do the readings in advance. Why do so, when the professor will simply explain to you in class what you need to know?

The research on the flipped classroom tells us that what makes it such an effective teaching strategy is the fact that students get the opportunity to *practice* and *receive immediate feedback on* the skills that they will need for the course assessments. As Susan Ambrose and her colleagues point out in *How Learning Works,* "[g]enerally speaking, both professors and students underestimate the need for practice" in the acquisition of new intellectual or creative skills. As faculty, we often assume that modeling the techniques for problem solving on the board or having students complete a problem or two in class will provide the students with the skills they need to succeed on their assessments. Ambrose and her colleagues note that faculty typically "move from concept to concept or skill to skill rather quickly, giving students no more than a single opportunity to practice each."[16] But the research on how students develop mastery of a skill tells us that students need multiple opportunities both to practice any skill they are trying to learn, and they need to receive targeted feedback in order to help them improve those skills from one practice session to the next. The simplest analogy, used by Ambrose and her colleagues, is to learning a musical instrument. Just as novice musicians must spend many hours practicing basic skills like playing scales or mastering difficult passages—and frequently do so in the presence of their teacher, receiving immediate and individualized feedback—so must our students spend many hours practicing the basic intellectual skills of our discipline. The flipped classroom offers precisely this opportunity: instead of sending students away to struggle in their dorm rooms on problems that you have modeled for them once in class, in the absence of any direct guidance or feedback from the instructor, you are giving them those multiple opportunities to practice problem solving (or whatever skill you are teaching) in your presence, and with your direct (one on one) or indirect (whole class) guidance. That practice time both helps them improve on the skill and gives them a clearer metacognitive picture of their learning.

The language of problem solving might seem more appropriate to STEM disciplines than to humanities or other qualitative courses, but that absolutely does not have to be the case. Whenever I teach a course that involves writing, one of my main objectives is always to help students learn to compose effective introductions to whatever genre of essay they are writing. In my early years of teaching, I would have students read several model essays, and then in class we would look at the first paragraphs of all of those essays, talk about which ones seemed most effective, and categorize them into different strategy types. Then I would let them know that they needed to follow one of those exemplary models and write a great introduction to their next paper, and I sent them away to do so on their own. Gradually, however, I realized that the students' introductions never quite lived up to my expectations. I was not giving them enough help in accomplishing this task. So a few years into my teaching career I started to teach this skill differently. When the students had an assignment due, I still asked them to read the introductions to several different essays, and we still analyzed them (albeit more briefly) and categorized them into different strategy types. But then I asked them to take out a blank of piece of paper and write an introduction to a paper with an approaching due date, again following one of the exemplary models we had just read. While they wrote, I circulated around the classroom, giving individual pointers to students. When they had finished, I asked them to turn the paper over and write another introduction, following another one of the models we had studied. Again I walked among them, working with individual students. This single practice session in the classroom probably still does not give them enough focused practice on this specific skill, but it definitely made a positive impact in the quality of their introductions, and it inspired me to adopt similar studio-style class sessions for teaching skills like incorporating quotations into a sentence and writing concluding paragraphs.

Flipping the classroom helps learning, but it also has tremendous potential to reduce cheating in your courses as well. That happens primarily because of the way in which the flipped classroom improves students' metacognitive awareness of their learning in the course. The benefits extend both to students who are grossly overconfident in their learning and to students who are underconfident, with the kind of low self-efficacy I describe in Chapter 2. First, as we saw in the case of the MIT physics students, cheating students were overconfident and poor judges of how much time and preparation they needed to complete the online homework problems. Most of them waited until the hours immediately prior to the deadline, and cheating levels increased as that witching hour approached. No doubt we should attribute some of that cheating to students who were lazy, had poor time management skills, were inveterate procrastinators, or were planning to cheat all along and just waited until the last minute to do it. But if that accounted for much or even most of the cheating taking place in those final hours, then the change to the course format would not have reduced the cheating in the online assessments. So we can surmise that poor metacognition, especially in the form of overconfidence in their ability to complete the problems within a given time period, accounted for a substantive amount of that homework copying, and that increased time practicing homework problems in class accounted for a substantive reduction in that cheating. Students who had the opportunity to work on the problems in class gained an immediate understanding of how difficult they were, and of how much time they took to complete. A student who had not had this opportunity would get the first set of problems without that knowledge, and hence could badly miscalculate.

But in the second case, for students who are plagued with low self-efficacy, classroom practice would increase their confidence in their ability to do the homework problems, especially if they are receiving immediate and ongoing feedback from the instructor or teaching assistants in those sessions. As a reminder, we can break down the concept of student self-efficacy into two parts: outcome expectancies, which, as Susan Ambrose and her colleagues explain, "reflect the belief that specific actions will bring about a desired outcome";[17] and efficacy expectancies, which "represent the belief that one is *capable* of identifying, organizing, initiating, and executing a course of action that will bring about a desired outcome."[18] Put together, these two expectancies mean that, in order to feel sufficiently motivated to undertake a difficult challenge, "a student must not only believe that doing the assigned work can earn a passing grade, she must also believe that she is capable of doing the work necessary to earn a passing grade."[19] The first of these beliefs relates to students' perception of the fairness of the evaluation criteria of the course. We can help students with this perception in the ways that Stephen Chew identified in his description of his clicker activities— by explaining to students that the low-stakes assessments undertaken in class are the same kinds of assessments that they will encounter in their graded work, and by evaluating that work fairly and transparently.

The second belief presents us with a more complex challenge: how do we convince students that they are capable of doing what we ask of them? In their list of recommendations to help faculty members meet this challenge, Ambrose and her colleagues provide the following key suggestion: to "provide early success opportunities."

Expectations for future performance are influenced by past experiences. Hence, early success can build a sense of efficacy. This strategy is incredibly important in courses that are known as "gateway" or "high-risk" course[s] or for students who come into your course with anxiety for whatever reason. For example, you might incorporate early, shorter assignments that account for a small percentage of the final grade but provide a sense of competence and confidence before you assign a larger project.[20]

This is precisely what problem-solving sessions in the remodeled physics courses accomplished, and what low-stakes assessments in any course will help accomplish as well. Giving students confidence in their ability to successfully meet the challenges of the course, as well as a better awareness of the time and effort they need to expend in order to do so, should go a long way toward improving metacognition in your students—and an equally long way in reducing the kind of cheating through desperation that comes from hopeless or hopelessly lost students.

If you work with students on a regular basis in the classroom, you will gain a clearer and more accurate picture of their knowledge and skills in the course material before the assessment is due. Suppose you give a first assignment of the semester, and you have not had any opportunity to see the students' work or assess their abilities prior to receiving the assignment. Unless you spot some obvious plagiarism, you have no way of knowing whether the abilities demonstrated by the students on the assignment match what they are capable of. I know that in my discipline we frequently rely on our familiarity with the particular writing style and skill level of each student in order to help us spot possible cheating. Students might suddenly turn in a far more sophisticated essay than they have shown themselves capable of producing, or even far more sophisticated sentences or phrases than they have employed previously, and these tip us off to the possibility of plagiarism. But this strategy only becomes effective later in the semester, when we become familiar with students' capabilities. Students could easily get around this informal plagiarism detection method by plagiarizing or cheating on their assignments right from the beginning of the course. As long as they kept a low profile in class—so as not to reveal their true abilities in discussion or lecture questions—they could plagiarize or even purchase essays for the course throughout the entire semester. This will *not* work, however, if you have spent time individually supervising and guiding students from the first through the very last class session.

An even better guarantee to ensure that students are doing their own work on your out-of-class assignment is to require them to either begin or complete part of it *during class time.* So let's say I asked my students to turn in those two introductory paragraphs they wrote in class for a writing exercise grade. I would give them a quick glance and ask students to revise one of them and use it as the actual opening of the upcoming paper assignment—*and to turn in the original version they wrote in class with the final paper,* so I can see how they revised and improved it. I can absolutely guarantee, in that case, that at least one of the paragraphs in that paper will not be plagiarized. But I would also know that, in addition to the introductory paragraph, the main idea for the paper—which they need to have in their heads in order to write their introduction—has come from them as well. (This will only work if I have told them in advance that they will be settling on their paper topic in class that day, since I would not want them to have to improvise a paper topic without time to think about it.) Giving students time to work on pieces of your assignment in class, or asking them to develop the initial or main idea of an assignment, should be compatible with just about any kind of assignment or material. If you are helping students learn how to write a research paper in your discipline, spend thirty minutes teaching them what they need to write a literature review, and then have them bring in hard copies of three sources and begin writing their literature review in class. If students are working on a group presentation in pairs, spend thirty minutes modeling what an effective presentation slide looks like, and then have them work with their partner to create three slides in class. Ideally, you would hold them accountable for this in-class work in some way: have them turn in the material they wrote in class with their final paper, or have them send you the slides they created. A quick glance at them, when you are grading the final product, will help you identify discrepancies substantive enough to indicate potential cheating.

Many professors might protest that they have only a few hours a week in which to present their course material. If students work on their projects during class time, will you have to gut essential course content? Maybe—but remember that while you may have lots of material to cover in your class, just because you are covering it doesn't mean that students are learning it. Any good lecturer knows that the material will be better absorbed if reduced to a few main ideas that are repeated over and over again. So, likewise, a good teacher should know that simply battering students with as much information as possible over the course of a semester will produce nothing but frustration for both teacher and student. It can be difficult indeed to let go of material that you feel is absolutely essential for a student in your course to have—I understand completely and feel your pain. But you will be doing your students a much greater service by reducing the amount of material that you are covering and actually ensuring that students are learning it, rather than making sure that you are ticking off every checkpoint on your ideal syllabus. Learning comes from practice, and you have to help and teach your students to practice just as you help and teach them the basic knowledge and skills of your discipline.

Before we conclude this chapter, I want to introduce you to our final guide, who convinced me that the ways in which we communicate with our students can also help them develop an appropriately gauged sense of self-efficacy. Joe Ben Hoyle is an associate professor of accounting at the University of Richmond who has won multiple accolades for his teaching over the course of a career that has lasted more than forty years, including an invitation by the students at the University of Richmond to deliver the school's inaugural "Last Lecture" in the spring of 2009. I first met Joe when he sent me a copy of his self-published book on teaching, and a link to his blog. Although I have an innate—and perhaps unwarranted—suspicion of self-published manuscripts sent to me in the mail, something about this one caught my attention, and I sat down and read it cover to cover. The ways in which Joe Ben Hoyle described helping his students learn were striking and original, and led me to profile Hoyle's reflections on teaching in a column for the *Chronicle of Higher Education*.[21] And although Hoyle has sharp insights into the job of teaching in a wide variety of areas, I believe he offers a truly inspiring model of communicating with his students to foster their self-efficacy and inspire them to learn.[22]

Indeed, what first really grabbed my attention, and continues to strike me as both an excellent reflection of Hoyle's teaching style and a wonderful teaching innovation, is presented at the outset of that book. Hoyle explains that, at the end of each semester, he sends an email to all of the students in his course who received an A. That email contains his congratulations for their effort and success in the course, and then asks a favor of the students: Hoyle asks them to describe the study strategies they used that allowed them to achieve the grade they earned. Although he uses their responses to help him determine whether he should make any changes to the course—if students are earning A's by all-night cramming, for example, he knows he wants to make changes to the exams—what distinguishes Hoyle's method as an model for building self-efficacy in his students comes next.

> All of the [student responses] are . . . cut and pasted into a single document which is distributed to the next class of students on the first day of the following semester. It is one handout that they read with interest and care; they are always inclined to believe the words of their fellow students. These short essays help remove any rumors or mystery associated with my class. From the beginning, I want every student to understand exactly what it takes to earn an excellent grade. In most team sports, the players who are seniors are expected to teach the freshmen what it means to be part of the team. That is what I am seeking: One group of students instructs the next on how to achieve excellence.[23]

I will note without comment that in fifteen years of teaching I have never communicated a congratulations to students who did well in the course or on the final exam, although I have often intended to. That Hoyle makes this a regular part of his teaching practice speaks volumes about his dedication both to his profession and to his students. But, more important, it reflects an awareness on his part that students need both tools and encouragement to succeed. We all work to give them the tools they need to succeed—we hope—in the ways in which we teach our courses, but how many of us think to give them encouragement in the way that this note does? The special genius of this note is not that it says "You can do it!" It says, instead, "You can do it—and I have evidence to show you that. Others just like you have done it before."

    If you scan through Hoyle's writing about teaching, and the articles that have been written about his teaching, I would argue that you will find three essential threads that characterize his communication with his students, and that I believe can help create the kind of self-efficacy we want in our students. The first of these sentiments relates as much to fostering intrinsic motivation as it does to communication, but it strikes me as an essential piece of the package that we find in Joe Ben Hoyle's work; the second and third thread twine together—and must twine together—to foster the self-efficacy our students need.

I Have Something Wonderful to Teach You

This sentiment shines through almost every piece of writing Hoyle shares with his students—and, I would imagine, his presence in the classroom as well. I haven't studied formally anything related to mathematics or the business world for a good twenty years now, but reading through Hoyle's descriptions of his discipline to his students makes me want to audit his Intermediate Accounting II class, the course I will focus on for the remainder of the chapter. Remember that, as we saw in Chapter 4, students are both less likely to cheat and more likely to learn when they see the course material as intrinsically fascinating, useful, or beautiful. Hoyle works hard and continually to help his students see his course in this way. In the most recent iteration of the course, for example, he began the process of sharing his genuine love for his course material, and helping his students learn to love it as well, several months before the semester started. In April of 2012, after the students had registered for their fall courses, Hoyle sent an email to all of the students on the roster in the Fall 2012 section of Intermediate Accounting II. His email spends several paragraphs telling the students about what the course will entail, and offering advice about how to succeed by doing some simple review work over the summer. But it moves beyond those simple practical messages. In this course, he explains to them, "[w]e cover some of the most interesting topics in all of accounting." That brief phrase prepares the way for a later section of the email, a final piece of advice to the students that encourages them to think about the larger world of business in which the course material exists, both because it will help them in the course and because it is an inherently fascinating topic of study. Over the summer, he exhorts them,

> keep up with the world of business. School should not be separate from the real world. (Did you know that Wal-Mart disclosed this morning that it had legal risks because of possible bribery in Mexico—what does that mean to the company?) . . . The study of the business world is like the study of a gigantic game with many interlocking pieces. The people who are successful in business understand the game and play it very well. The more you learn about business the more you realize that there is so much more to learn. It is not just a way to get a first job; being in business should be an adventure. And, the more you learn in college, the better that adventure will be.

The enthusiasm for the world of business and accounting that shines through this paragraph infects everything that Hoyle writes to his students. I love the parenthetical aside about Walmart: Here's something in the daily news that relates to our subject matter—let's think about what it means! Business as a game, as an adventure, as a context that connects their studies with the world around them—all of these words and phrases and ideas help convince students that, in Hoyle's course, they are participating in something worth learning.

That attitude continues into the semester when Hoyle actually meets the students for the first time and presents his syllabus to them. I can hardly imagine a course that sounds more like it would induce thoughts of mechanical learning than Intermediate Accounting II. Hoyle makes it very clear to them on his syllabus that such will not be the case in his course. While naturally they will be doing computations and other seemingly mechanical activities, the real focus of the course lies with thinking about and understanding the practice of accounting. As his syllabus puts it:

> Sherlock Holmes would have been a wonderful accountant because he constantly pounded himself with the question "What happened here and why?" 2 plus 2 is 4 is mechanical knowledge that can be learned with little or no thought. Why accounting works in a particular fashion is not mechanical and takes serious contemplation to truly understand. People who don't do well in Intermediate Accountings tend to be obsessed with the mechanics rather than with the "why."

Hoyle's course, by contrast, will always keep that larger picture in view, encouraging students to think about the meanings behind the numbers. They will engage in "serious contemplation." And, indeed, he explains to them that the main purpose of the course is not learning to crunch numbers, or even really just to understand accounting more thoroughly. The main purpose of this course, like every course he teaches, is much more fundamental:

> I feel that you will hold a competitive advantage in life if you obtain a basic understanding of financial accounting. More importantly, I believe you will be more likely to make something of yourself if you learn to think . . . In this class, we use financial accounting simply as a means for stimulating your ability to think and reason.

Maintaining the focus of the students on the larger picture of the business world, and on the fundamental thinking skills that will help them live richer lives, no doubt helps maintain their interest in the subject matter when they find themselves slogging through the more mechanical tasks of accounting—or of any discipline, for that matter. I tend to assume that the relationship of literature to larger questions of meaning and value should be apparent in all aspects of my courses, but I suspect students might disagree with that when I am holding their noses to a poem—or tying it to a chair, in the words of the poet Billy Collins—and asking them to identify the various forms of figurative language they find in there. Hoyle continually asks his students to step back from the smaller mechanical tasks and take a look at the complex and fascinating whole—to think about accounting, about business, and about thinking itself. I love this stuff, his messages to the students imply—and you will too!

I Am Going to Challenge You

In addition to the five times he has won the University of Richmond's Distinguished Educator Award, in the spring of 2005 the senior business majors at the university voted him the "Most Feared Professor" on campus. As a result of this interesting distinction, the university's alumni magazine invited him to contribute an essay on his teaching philosophy. He concludes that essay with a remark that captures well his convictions about challenging students: "Our students can do amazing things, but if we don't challenge them fully, they will never realize what marvelous talents they truly possess."[24] In the introductory email to his students in the spring, he addresses right away the impression students probably already have that his course will prove "fully" challenging. Intermediate Accounting II, he says to them, "is not a course to be taken lightly." And that same language continues on the syllabus when students arrive, where Hoyle explains to them that good students will achieve much in his course, but "achievement does not come without sacrifice." He then explains what that sacrifice will look like, and why he asks it of them:

> Proper preparation is the key to achievement whether you are trying to get a team ready to win the World Series or the Super Bowl or earn an A+ in this course. There is just a right way and a wrong way to do things. I expect you to arrive at class every day having thought about the material and being ready to explore it with me. Don't expect to come to class and just take notes as I pass out pearls of wisdom. That's not learning—that's memorization. I'll ask questions and I'll expect answers, answers based on your preparation and your ability to think.

This explanation is essential to the structure of the course, which Hoyle teaches in a completely Socratic fashion. He poses at least one question to every student in class every day. Students have to undertake the kind of preparation he describes here in order both for his teaching style to work, and for them to receive the benefits of a Socratic teaching style—engaging with difficult questions, thinking for oneself, challenging and being challenged by the other thinkers in the room. When so many college courses still rely primarily on lectures or discussions in which participation is optional, you can imagine how his teaching style represents a full challenge to today's college student.

We might expect that a teacher who conducts his class by discussion, and who values it so highly, would include some kind of participation grade in the course, as many of us do. We would be wrong. "I don't see any reason at all to reward something that's simply expected," Hoyle said in an interview about his teaching with *BusinessWeek* magazine. "I don't reward breathing. I don't reward participation." We might also expect that participatory classes like this one allow for plenty of opportunity for the teacher to dish out praise to student comments, reinforcing the "good job" phenomenon I described at the outset of this chapter. But praise comes only to those who earn it. "I say, 'Good job!,'" Hoyle explains in his article in the alumni magazine, "when a student gives me a thoughtful, well-conceived answer." But, unlike me on the softball field, he does not simply hand out 'Good job' praise for any contribution: "I say, 'Listen, you can do better than that!' when a student gives me a bad answer." And when students consistently come to class unprepared, or do not give the kinds of answers he expects from them, they do not get a break either, as he explains in his teaching tips book: "If any students consistently fail to prepare, I call them in and we discuss the advantages of being able to provide and support answers."[25] Notice the way in which, in the case of students who are not doing the preparatory work they need in order to succeed in class, Hoyle avoids browbeating them, and instead focuses the message on the importance of students continuing to challenge themselves: *you can do better than that*, rather than *you did poorly*; and *here's why preparation helps you in this course*. And notice as well that, for students who consistently underperform, Hoyle calls them into his office and talks to them about how to succeed in the course, rather than simply giving up on them.

Hoyle's confidence in his students' abilities leads us to the second half of the sentence that began this section. *I am going to challenge you*, that sentence began; it finishes like this:

You Are Capable of Meeting that Challenge

Joe Ben Hoyle may hammer away at this point more than any other in his written and face-to-face communications with students. It appears in every document he sent to me in one form or another. "I honestly want Intermediate Accounting II to be the best course you have ever taken," he tells them in his pre-course email. "If I do my job really well and if you do your job really well, we can achieve that goal . . . with a good effort from both of us, you are more than capable of handling that challenge." His eight-page syllabus concludes with the following exhortation, in all capital letters: "BELIEVE IN YOURSELF—YOU REALLY CAN DO THIS STUFF!!!" In the document that he gives to his new students about how to achieve an A in class, compiled from students who have done so in previous semesters, his introduction to that advice includes the following sentences: "I want to help you ratchet up your game. To me, that is as important as learning accounting. I really do want you to learn how to be successful when faced with a genuine challenge." Follow the advice of these wise students, Hoyle continues, and "I guarantee you what they say can form a road map for your getting an A."

Do we really need to offer this kind of cheerleading to our students? If you are not going to challenge them, you probably do not. If you are going to challenge them, you not only need to offer them exhortations like these, but you need to back up the exhortations with concrete advice about how they can meet the challenges you set for them. Hoyle does not rely exclusively on the wisdom of past students to help his current students. The entire second half of Hoyle's eight-page syllabus provides advice for students on how to do well in the course. It contains the usual material you might find on any syllabus about putting in the time on the reading and homework and so on. But you will also find sharp and interesting comments like these:

A lot of students like to gather in the Atrium 30–45 minutes before my classes just to sit and discuss the handouts. I think that is wonderful. I think that really helps. They always walk into class ready to go. If I could, I would require that. Absolutely!!! However, do me a personal favor. If there are people in the atrium from our class, include everyone in the conversation. Some people are quiet and don't want to butt in. I want everyone in the class to become part of the group. Don't be snooty. You make the move to be friendly. Look around—is there anyone there that you can ask to "come on over and help us talk about this accounting nonsense."

What I think deserves particular notice in this paragraph—aside from the excellent advice for students to engage in these informal study sessions before class—is the fact that Hoyle encourages them to engage with each other in an ethical and generous way. You see this ethic of generosity in everything he writes to his students, or writes about his teaching. We're all in this together, he seems to say—so let's all help each other succeed.

And when Hoyle implies to the students that "we" are all in this together, he casts a wide and generous net. Consider an email that Hoyle sends—brace yourself—to the *parents* of the students who are enrolled in his class. At the beginning of the semester, Hoyle asks the students in his course to give him the email addresses of their parents, if—and only if—they would like to receive occasional updates from him on the course that their son or daughter is taking. (The parents can choose to opt out after the first email.) As Hoyle explains in the email, he began doing this after he sent his own children to college and was distressed at how little he knew about what was happening in their daily educational lives. And while Hoyle's message does provide the parents with information about the course, the bulk of it actually focuses on providing tips for parents on how they can help their son or daughter succeed in the course. "When your child is at home," he writes, "talk with them about your job or your investments or a business story that you read in the paper or just anything having to do with business." So the parents get a taste of the same enthusiasm for business and accounting that Hoyle shares with his students. But they also get some friendly advice about parenting any student through a difficult learning experience: "Never fail to tell your child that you are proud of him/her for doing the work; tell your child that you know there is a lot required but it is only for 3 months or so and that the work will really make them better. One of the hardest jobs that I have is convincing students that the hours of work before each class really are worth the effort—and you can help." Anyone who has parented a child through multiple levels of education—and I have five of them, so I speak from long and sometimes painful experience—knows how badly they need to hear that message from us sometimes. I wonder whether I ever would have thought to continue speaking it to my soon-to-be-college-aged children without this reflection from Joe Hoyle.

In *How Learning Works*, Susan Ambrose and her colleagues point out that one of the best means we can use to help improve students' sense of self-efficacy is to provide the kind of strategic advice that Hoyle gives to his students (and their parents!). Especially in challenging classes, they explain, "[s]tudents may not be able to identify ways in which they should appropriately change their study behaviors following failure . . . it is important to discuss effective study strategies to give them alternatives to the behaviors that resulted in poor performance."[26] When we communicate explicitly with our students about the strategies that will help them learn in our courses, we demystify what students might see as an impossible or baffling challenge. We have all heard students who say they are "bad at math," or "just can't write"; those beliefs demotivate students by implying that, no matter how hard they work or study, they will never succeed. Providing them with concrete advice for how to succeed in a course or a discipline—from how to read your notes to how to meet before class—helps them see that learning depends on their effort instead of some innate learning skill that they were blessed with (or not blessed with) at birth. Remember that the MIT physicists also noted that the pathway to success in their course was not some inborn scientific intelligence, but doing the homework. When we communicate these notions clearly to our students, we are giving them the tools they need to succeed—and in doing so, are removing one more reason they might have to cheat.

PART THREE

SPEAKING ABOUT CHEATING

Although the most effective means we have to reduce cheating in our courses lie within our own hands, of course cheating does occur within a larger campus context. And the fifth contextual condition that leads to greater cheating—when students perceive that their peers either are cheating around them or approve of cheating—may lend itself equally well to remedies established by the instructor and to ones constructed in the campus environment as a whole. In this final part of the book, we will turn to the ways in which both individual instructors and campus leaders—administrators, staff members, and student leaders—can speak effectively to students on campus about cheating, in the hopes of reducing cheating at the course and campus-wide level. Almost none of what we have covered thus far involves speaking with students explicitly about the topic of academic integrity and cheating. When we move into academic integrity policies, and honor codes, and sanctions for violators, we are considering all of the ways in which we speak to students about cheating. What do we say to students about cheating? How often do we say it? And in what venues?

Before we enter upon that discussion, I want to note the first and most fundamental reason that every campus has to speak about cheating: to settle upon a definition of cheating that governs the campus, and to invite all members of the campus community into that conversation. If you page your way through a half-dozen academic integrity policies available online,[1] you will immediately see the problem with assuming (as many of us might) that we are working with shared standards of academic integrity as a profession. Consider just the following three statements.

1. From Stanford University, as an example of a violation of their honor code: "Giving or receiving aid on an academic assignment under circumstances in which a reasonable person should have known that such aid was not permitted."

2. From the University of Texas at Austin's description of "Unauthorized Collaboration": "The instructor—not the student —determines the purpose of a particular assignment *and* the acceptable method for completing it. Unless working together on an assignment has been specifically authorized, always assume it is not allowed."

3. From Syracuse University's Academic Integrity Policy: "The instructor of record is responsible for determining and communicating course-specific academic integrity expectations. Instructors of record are responsible for stating course-specific expectations in writing, particularly those regarding use of sources and collaboration."

I will take a page from Stanley Fish's playbook here and point out that in statements like these, as in many institutional policy statements you will find about academic integrity, we can see how much a definition of cheating varies according to the local interpretive community, both from campus to campus and from course to course.[2] While we all might agree that cutting and pasting material from Wikipedia without any attribution counts as plagiarism—unless, perhaps, you have just cut and pasted the birthdate of George Washington?—the actual determination of what counts as academic dishonesty can vary according to both the institution and the instructor. As Tricia Bertram Gallant has pointed out, in today's "diverse institutions" we may find "multiple and conflicting ideas of acceptable classroom conduct and legitimate academic work."[3] So we absolutely cannot take it for granted that faculty (and students and administrators) at any institution join their particular interpretive academic community with a shared understanding of what counts as cheating. And I would suggest further that the varying standards we see from institution to institution suggest that attempting to discover a universally applicable definition of academic cheating is a quixotic task. Cheating is like a weed; a weed is any plant you don't want in your garden, and cheating is any practice that the campus community and instructor have forbidden. What counts as cheating in your course may be different from what counts as cheating in mine.[4] We can't hold students to standards of academic integrity that we haven't clearly established.

I know that most institutions have an academic integrity policy of some kind, one that likely establishes a general set of standards for the entire campus, and that you will find on the website somewhere or in the student handbook. And while that general set of standards should apply to all classes, as an instructor I still have my own decisions to make about the areas in which the policy leaves decisions up to me—such as whether I allow collaboration on homework, or allow students to submit work for my class that they have completed in another class. One of the problems that I believe contributes to a cheating environment stems from a lack of coordination between the campus policy and individual instructors. If individual instructors are either not fully aware of the policies, or circumvent or ignore them in their courses, that sends a powerful message to students, one that perhaps suggests to them that academic integrity standards don't matter as much in some courses as in others. So one of the most important tasks we have as a campus community is to speak with a clear and powerful voice to students about academic integrity, and to clarify for them as much as possible the ways in which it manifests itself both in the broader environ-ment and in individual classes.

As you will see in what follows, much of the conversation about cheating that I believe we must have will take place among ourselves—before we can speak to our students about cheating, we must speak to each other about it.

8

CHEATING ON CAMPUS

One of the most publicly visible and easily graspable methods that an institution of higher education possesses to speak with its students about cheating comes in the form of the traditional honor code. A traditional honor code places the responsibility for academic integrity in the hands of the students, by requiring each incoming class to pledge loyalty to a code of behavior on their academic work—typically a code that students have authored or co-authored, and have the responsibility for maintaining and administering. According to a white paper by Timothy Dodd, a former Director of the International Center for Academic Integrity, such traditional honor codes will typically include "three or more" of the following features:

student initiated and operated
students have full responsibility for investigation, adjudication, and sanctioning
impose a single sanction for all violations (suspension or expulsion)
include a nontoleration clause (duty to report violations); failure of a witness to report a violation is a violation
require a signed pledge on all work submitted
all students must pass an honor code test or participate in honor code education before academic work will be graded.[1]

So in a traditional honor code environment, students who have violated their pledge may find themselves facing a jury of their peers, and guilty parties are subject to uniformly imposed punishments that are well known to all students in advance. Traditional honor codes also typically place the burden of reporting violations on the students themselves. So faculty members at a code institution might leave their exams unproctored, but students who witness a student cheating in an unproctored exam are expected, as part of their fealty to the code, to report such violations to the appropriate governing body. *Not* reporting a witnessed violation, in a traditional honor code environment, counts as a violation itself.

A substantial amount of research has been done on the effectiveness of such codes, and much of it points to the possibility that codes do offer a potent means of reducing cheating on campus. Donald McCabe, the leading contemporary researcher on cheating whose work we reviewed in Chapter 1, has long been an advocate for the traditional honor code as a means of creating a campus environment that reduces student cheating. So, for example, he and Patrick Drinan pointed out, in a 1999 opinion piece in the *Chronicle of Higher Education,* that campuses with traditional honor codes have been documented as having lower cheating rates than noncode schools: "on campuses with honor codes, fewer than one in 14 students surveyed in the 1995–96 academic year acknowledged cheating repeatedly on tests and examinations, compared with one in six at institutions without honor codes."[2] Such statistical data represent a continuation of findings by William J. Bowers, the author of the first major cheating survey in 1963, who likewise found that self-reported rates of cheating at schools with traditional honor codes were lower than at noncode schools. Many writers who address the topic of cheating in higher education have picked up on such statistics and argue or imply that campuses should begin their fight against cheating by instituting an honor code of some type or another.

Not all of us, however, are quite convinced. Honor codes

have traditionally faced some major challenges, the most difficult of which has come in the form of the expectation that students will report on one another if they witness code violations. In the fall of 2011, I made a visit to Oxford College at Emory University, a two-year liberal arts college that students elect to attend prior to shifting to the larger campus at Emory for their third and fourth years. I had the opportunity to meet with the student members of the Honors Council at Oxford, the group that administers their traditional honor code, both to hear their concerns and to offer advice on potential modifications to their code. The number one concern that the council members expressed to me was students' failure to report on one another. Even when a student had been reported for committing a violation, and the Council called in his or her peers to gather more information, they found themselves frequently faced with uncooperative or willfully blind students.

They are not alone in that experience. In one of McCabe's large-scale surveys, he found that only 1 percent of students at honor code institutions reported that "their code influences students to report cheaters."[3] The students cited a wide range of reasons for the reluctance of students to report on peer violations:

> a fear of being responsible for having another student expelled, a fear of making an enemy, a concern about reporting on a friend, a fear that the accused student might actually be innocent, a code of silence that exists in some honor code environments based on the sentiment that squealing is worse than cheating, peer intimidation associated with the code of silence, and a fear that the instructor or administrators will not be able or willing to prosecute the offender.[4]

None of this should come as a surprise to us, once we remind ourselves (again) that we are dealing with human beings in their late teens and early twenties, when peer approval looms so large in their lives. Remember that we know that cheating occurs more frequently when students perceive their peers cheating or believe that their peers approve of their cheating. It seems a bit quixotic to me to hope that we can address that problem by suddenly expecting students to shrug off their relationships with their peers and report them for honor code violations—especially when doing so might potentially result in their peers being suspended or expelled from campus, impacting their lives forever.

At this point I will tip my own hand and argue that the responsibility for enforcement of academic honesty should not be the primary responsibility of students. Again I would simply note that academic dishonesty happens in the courses that we design, that we are teaching, and that we have the responsibility for administering. If students are cheating in our classes, we should take primary responsibility for discovering that and responding to it. I think it makes little sense to place that burden on the backs of eighteen-year-old students, whose moral and intellectual development may be in early formative stages (as documented by William Perry and many subsequent researchers in this area), and who have had neither the opportunity to think very deeply about the importance of academic honesty or the experiences in dealing with it that most faculty members will have. What seems like a clear ethical imperative to us—report on students who are breaking the honor code—might seem much less clear to our students. As the authors of *Cheating in School* rightly point out, what we see as a right-versus-wrong dilemma can appear to the student as a "right-versus-right choice when considering cheating."[5] It is right to follow the rules of academic integrity, but it is also right to show loyalty to one's peers. Asking eighteen-year-olds to understand and navigate correctly this complex moral code strikes me as the equivalent of pulling the average citizen off the street, requiring them to sign a pledge that they will follow the law, and then giving them a police uniform and a gun and asking them to start arresting their neighbors every time they see an infraction. *Should* they arrest their neighbors? Of course. But there can be no doubt that doing so will change the relationship between neighbor and neighbor, as well as the general environment of the neighborhood—and not always for the better, in spite of the small benefits it might have for academic integrity in general.

So for both practical and philosophical reasons, I believe that traditional honor codes are not the best means we have to talk to our students about academic dishonesty—and I would suggest in particular that schools that do not currently have codes should not expend the considerable time and effort it takes to construct one, with the hopes that it will reduce cheating. And yet, you might be wondering, how can you discount the fact that cheating rates at honor code institutions have been consistently reported as lower than rates at code institutions?

To answer that question, I want to point to a key finding by McCabe and his co-author Linda Klebe Trevino in their discussion of a large-scale survey on cheating that took place during the 1990–1991 academic year, and that they reported in *The Journal of Higher Education* in 1993. I will quote the paragraph in its entirety:

> Interestingly, in the present research one of the lowest rates of self-reported academic dishonesty was found at a non-honor code institution. However, this institution is strongly committed to the concept of academic honor, making it a major topic of discussion in its student handbook and at orientation sessions for incoming students, where it goes to great lengths to ensure that its policy is understood and that academic honor is the obligation of every member of the campus community. At the other ex-

treme, one of the higher incidences of unethical behavior was found at a school with a long-standing honor code. However, students reported a low level of understanding and acceptance of the school's policy and the official with primary responsibility for administering the honor code supported this finding by suggesting that the institution has diminished its efforts in communicating and implementing its code in recent years.[6]

I draw two conclusions from this finding. First, what reduces cheating on an honor code campus is not the code itself, but *the dialogue about academic honesty that the code inspires*. In other words, codes provide multiple opportunities for an institution to speak to students about academic honesty, and multiple ways to engage them in that dialogue. Students have to be educated about the code at orientation; they have written versions of it in their handbooks and online; they are reminded about the code when they turn in their assignments or exams and have to sign a pledge. Students on code campuses have constant reminders about the importance of academic honesty, and those reminders—rather than the code itself—help reduce their cheating. Hence the noncode school which makes academic honesty "a major topic of discussion," as McCabe and Trevino put it, can see the same levels of reduced cheating that one can find at a traditional honor code institution.

Second, and equally important, *institutions do not need an honor code in order to foster the kind of campus discussion that will reduce cheating*; they can achieve that same end through other types of campus dialogues. As long as an institution makes a concerted effort to speak about cheating with its students, as the first institution described above seems to do, and to provide them with regular reminders of their obligations toward academic dishonesty, a code might prove entirely superfluous. In the second institution discussed in the paragraph above, it seems clear that an honor code without campus dialogue about academic dishonesty has little effect in reducing cheating.

A trio of researchers at Midwestern State University reported on a twenty-year study of cheating at their institution that provides further evidence for this conclusion. The authors looked at cheating rates on campus as measured by surveys conducted in 1984, 1994, and 2004. (Consistent with the research that we considered in Chapter 1, the authors did not see a massive increase in cheating during that time period; overall rates of cheating crept up from 54.1 percent in 1984 to 57.4 percent in 2004.) During the 2002–2003 academic year, Midwestern State adopted a student-authored and -instituted honor code. Hence the authors were especially interested to see whether the new honor code would reduce the rates of cheating on campus, as the research of McCabe and others (which they cite) would suggest. Their findings did not reveal what you might expect: "student awareness of an honor code with broad university support did not reduce cheating in our study."[7] The authors suggest that one possible reason for this lack of an effect may be that the very recent adoption of the code had not allowed enough time for a rich campus dialogue about academic dishonesty to flourish. That may yet happen, of course, but for our purposes their findings confirm the notion that the dialogue about academic honesty inspired by a code, not the code itself, provides the key to reducing cheating on campus.

And indeed, if you look beyond the quick statistical data you will find in cheating surveys comparing honor code and noncode institutions, you will usually find an acknowledgement along these lines, even among the most ardent supporters of the honor code model. So McCabe and Trevino concede, in their 1993 essay in *The Journal of Higher Education,* that "any movement to adopt honor codes is ill conceived if it is undertaken as the sole solution to the academic dishonesty problem."[8] Or

McCabe and Patrick Drinan, in their 1999 opinion piece in the *Chronicle of Higher Education*: "Honor codes, in and of themselves, are not the only means to mitigate cheating at colleges and universities. The success of honor codes appears to be rooted in a campus tradition of mutual trust and respect among students and between faculty members and students."[9] Or McCabe and Gary Pavela, in an editorial on "New Honor Codes for a New Generation" published on the insidehighered.com website in 2005: "The critical difference [between honor code and noncode campuses] seems to be an ongoing dialogue that takes place among students on campuses with strong honor code traditions, and occasionally between students and relevant faculty and administrators."[10] And finally, McCabe and his coauthors in *Cheating in College:* "the power of an honor code today appears to be directly related to how effectively students are oriented into this tradition and how much effort and resources a campus is willing to expend in working with faculty and students to institutionalize a code within its culture and keep it alive over time."[11] The implication made in all of these statements is that for an honor code to work, campuses must ensure that the code helps create a rich dialogue centered upon academic dishonesty. My review of this literature leads me to a different conclusion: forget about the code, and simply concentrate on creating the rich campus dialogue.

Please don't read this argument as suggesting that institutions with honor codes should repeal them and start from scratch. Honor codes *can* do an excellent job of stimulating dialogue about academic honesty, and they seem to be doing so at many institutions. But if you do not currently have an honor code at your institution, you are welcome to read this argument as a suggestion that you should not expend the time and effort you will need in order to construct one. Although traditional honor codes may be authored and administered by the students, helping students create a code will take considerable effort by a small group of faculty and administrators, and will need consistent oversight in order to function effectively.[12] That fact, coupled with the problematic feature of traditional codes—students being required to report on each other's violations—makes me unwilling to recommend them as a remedy for institutions seeking to address academic honesty issues at the campuswide level.

All right, I hope you are now thinking, we don't need an honor code—but how can we create that rich campus dialogue about academic honesty that we need to reduce cheating on our campus? And what should that dialogue consist of? Does it mean making students constantly aware of the punishments they will face if they are caught cheating? Does it mean continual exhortations to students to act in virtuous or honest ways? Advertisements for academic honesty in the campus newspaper? Posters in the hallway? Will talking about cheating in any context —such as debating the standards of academic honesty in a class or a public forum—provide the kind of dialogue that will help reduce cheating on campus, or do we have to continually remind them to act in the right way? Before I give my own set of concrete recommendations for constructing that dialogue, I want to introduce one final concept from the literature on human learning: *priming*.

As we have discussed already in Part II, asking our students to take the knowledge they have obtained in our classes and apply it in new and different contexts is one of the most difficult tasks for them—or for any learner—to achieve. As Susan Ambrose and her colleagues rightly note, we might think about students' ability to transfer knowledge from one context to another as "the central goal of education: we want our students to be able to apply what they learn beyond the classroom."[13] But much gets in the way of this happening. Students who learn to master a skill in one particular context often have great difficulty transferring it to a new and unfamiliar one. So in a media studies course you might work with your students on analyzing all of the ways in which a television ad seeks to manipulate them using various gender and race stereotypes; but when those same students are sitting home flipping through magazines, perusing the ads that make use of those same stereotypes, they might never think to apply the analytic tools they have picked up in your classes. This can happen because they think about the knowledge as too closely tied to the specific context in which they learn it, or because they have not learned it deeply enough. In any case, this kind of knowledge transfer probably doesn't happen nearly as often as we would either like or imagine it happens.

That doesn't mean we are useless in the face of the obstacles to knowledge transfer, however. One of the most important ways in which we can help students learn to transfer knowledge to new contexts is through the very simple technique of offering them reminders or prompts prior to their encountering that new context. So, for example, after you had analyzed a series of television commercials in class, if you suggest that students apply those same skills to the advertisements in the next magazine they read, they are much more likely to do so because of your suggestion. Ambrose and her colleagues document a fascinating example of this with students who read about and memorized a text about a complex military maneuver in which an army had to divide up and approach a target from multiple directions. When those students were presented afterward with "a medical problem that required a similar solution [approaching a tumor from multiple angles with laser beams] . . . the large majority of students did not apply what they had learned to the medical problem." When the students were prompted to apply the military strategy to the medical one, however, the majority of them *were* able to apply what they had learned from the military maneuver to the medical problem. "A little prompting, in other words," conclude Ambrose and her colleagues, "can go a long way in helping students apply what they know."[14]

Dan Ariely and his colleagues, in *The (Honest) Truth about Dishonesty,* ran an experiment that demonstrated a parallel phenomenon when students were confronting an ethical problem. Using the standard mathematical test that they constructed for many of their experiments, they took 450 lab subjects and divided them into two groups. The first group of subjects was asked to recall and write down as many of the Ten Commandments as possible; the second group was asked, by contrast, simply to remember and write down "ten books they had read in high school."[15] After they had completed these memory tasks, the two groups took the mathematics test, on which they were induced to cheat. The result: "Among the group who recalled the ten books, we saw the typical widespread but moderate cheating. On the other hand, in the group that was asked to recall the Ten Commandments, we observed no cheating whatsoever."[16] (This effect occurred even though none of the subjects had been able to correctly remember all of the Ten Commandments—which means that Ariely and his colleagues did not happen to group together a set of overly religious subjects.) Simply being reminded of a set of culturally specific religious tenets prior to their completing the test drastically reduced the amount of cheating.

The basic umbrella term that we can use for the phenomenon documented by both Ambrose and Ariely and their colleagues is *priming,* which refers simply to the way in which we can use prompts or reminders of previously learned knowledge or experiences to influence a person's response to new knowledge or experiences. Ariely's experiment, in particular, suggests that we can use priming not only to help learners transfer knowledge from one context to another, but to help human beings remember their ethical obligations when they are confronted with a challenging or difficult situation. Keep in mind, though, that timing proves crucial in creating effective priming. Ariely and his colleagues actually put this notion to the test by administering the cheating-inducing math test to students at Princeton University, who sign an honor code statement at the beginning of their freshman year and take what he describes as an intensive "crash course on morality" in relation to academic honesty during their freshman orientation. Two weeks after a group of Princeton freshman had completed their honor code training, he administered his standard math test; he gave the same test, at the same time, to students at Harvard University and MIT, neither of which have honor codes. When he compared the rates of cheating among the Princeton students two weeks after their honor code training to the rates of cheating among Harvard and MIT students who had received no such training, he found no differences whatsoever. Two weeks after their honor code training, Princeton students were just as likely to cheat on the math test as students who had not encountered such training. By contrast, when he asked students from all three schools to sign an "honor code" statement just prior to taking the math test, *none of them* cheated on the test. So what prevented cheating, in all cases, was a simple reminder about academic honesty just prior to the students' taking the test—and not some general effort to drill the virtues of academic honesty into students at the beginning of their freshman year.[17]

So what does all this tell us about how to create a campus dialogue about academic honesty on your campus, and about what that dialogue should look like (or perhaps sound like)? I would extrapolate four basic strategies from what we have learned thus far about honor codes, knowledge transfer, and priming, in order to give you and your colleagues just a little bit of help in constructing that dialogue, or working with your staff and administration and student leaders in order to construct that dialogue on campus.

Begin the Conversation among the Faculty

Keeping in mind the slippery nature of academic integrity (at least in some areas), and the fact that it might appear in different forms from one course to the next, the institution should establish some recurring opportunity for a team of faculty—perhaps joined by administrators and students—to gather together and revisit (and revise if necessary) the general academic integrity policy in light of the constantly evolving nature of intellectual work in the academic community. This might happen every year or three years or five years, but most of us have seen important changes in the types of information that are available to our students during our careers, and the methods that students use for gathering and attributing sources. That ongoing evolution seems unlikely to stop anytime soon. A regular revisiting of the policy will give the members of the community the chance to discuss and possibly revise those policies. It will also give the institution the opportunity to remind all members of the community about the existing (or newly revised) academic integrity policies, such as tenured faculty members like myself who don't normally think to sit down and reread them very often. Finally, it will benefit recently joined members of the community from all groups by allowing them to have a voice in the process, and educating them about the existing policies. Such a meeting could take many forms. If you have an academic integrity office on campus, or a teaching and learning center, those would seem like natural organizing places. At my institution, we don't have those offices, but we do have an open meeting of the faculty every semester for informal conversations about teaching, and we could easily use one of those meetings every few years in order to address this issue. The authors of *Cheating in School* suggest another interesting possibility: "Create a network of liaisons in departments who are champions of integrity and a resource for their close colleagues."[18] If each academic department on campus had an academic integrity liaison, those faculty members could form an academic integrity council charged with the responsibility of setting policy and educating and assisting their colleagues.

Given the increasing reliance of colleges and universities today on adjunct labor, it deserves noting that part-time faculty should either have a role in such a council or should be included in any academic integrity outreach activities. One group of researchers who surveyed part-time faculty on academic integrity issues and compared their responses to those of students and full-time faculty found that their academic integrity experiences and policies differed in some key ways from those of full-time faculty. For example, "part-time faculty are significantly less likely to sanction students who cheat." And while full-time faculty "are more likely to administer sanctions . . . they are also significantly more likely to educate students about integrity practices."[19] The authors of the study suggest that institutions could appoint an "ombudsman" for part-time faculty who could help them not only gain a clear sense of the institutional policy, but also serve as an aid or mediator for them when they are faced with academic integrity violations in their classrooms.[20]

One of the practical consequences that might come from such a meeting would be that faculty members learn to draw from the existing academic integrity policies of the institution in constructing their own course-specific policies. Even if you do not have the kind of regular meeting recommended above, you can still take this important step on your own. Because the definition of cheating can be a slippery one, varying from one learning environment to the next, faculty members who act outside of the policy will contribute to an already potentially confusing situation for undergraduate students. So course-specific policies should point back to the university policy, and should clarify for students when your policy aligns exactly with the campus policy and when it represents a choice on your part in response to an open-ended policy statement—such as the choice to allow collaboration on certain types of assignments, or the choice to allow students to revise papers they have written for other courses and turn them in for your course. Faculty members should help students navigate this tricky territory by making clear the source of their policies: those that come from a campus-wide handbook, for example, and those that apply only in their specific courses. This might also hold true for the expectations you have about citation and attribution, for the ways in which you respond to cheating in your courses, and for the expectations you have for students to report academic integrity violations. The source of all of your policies should be available for students—on your syllabus, for example, or a course website—just as you expect your students to make available to you the sources that contributed to their academic work.

Continue It Into the Community

Once the general academic integrity policies of the campus have been formulated and clarified, those policies must be broadcast to the community on a regular basis. The community should be invited into an ongoing conversation about the subject—and, potentially, participate in ongoing revision of the policy. As the authors of *Cheating in School* suggest, "*sustained* conversations [about academic integrity] are required to strengthen our academic institutions."[21] A meeting among faculty every few years obviously will not go far in creating a campus culture of academic integrity; the conversations must be ongoing, and must involve all affected members of the campus community. Typically the "conversations" about cheating on campus take the form of educational campaigns, which means they are going to be one-sided conversations in which campus leaders from all categories are working to educate students. That seems sensible enough to me, although what we know about human learning would suggest that we have to provide opportunities for students to engage actively with the ideas somehow. Such engagement could come in many forms, but before presenting one or two ideas along those lines I want to name the constituents who should play a role in constructing an academic integrity educational campaign.

First and foremost, faculty should play a major role in developing curricular aspects of an educational campaign on academic honesty standards, since those standards operate primarily in our classrooms. I don't believe we can abdicate this responsibility, or shrug it off onto some dedicated office of academic integrity. For those offices to have an impact, they need the support of faculty. The same faculty group that meets to review and revisit the academic integrity policies, as described above, could work to develop the content of an educational campaign, or it could come from a separately charged body. That group should first educate themselves about the best practices in helping students learn the standards of academic honesty and then help develop whatever materials or plans will be used with your students. Some quick online searching, for example, will turn up multiple quizzes designed to educate students about plagiarism. The School of Education at Indiana University in Bloomington has developed an online tutorial that students can walk through to learn about plagiarism.[22] It offers a clear and thorough overview of the issues involved, with plenty of examples for students to consider. Students can then take a practice test to see whether they have learned the material accurately, and then an online quiz, which tests their knowledge more thoroughly. Once they have completed the quiz with one hundred percent accuracy, they can view and print a certificate that they can turn into instructors or advisors at any institution. Many such tutorials and quizzes on plagiarism and academic honesty are available for free and fair use online. A faculty group that reviews and vets resources like this one can help make regular recommendations about them to their colleagues, who could decide whether or not to use them in their courses.

But faculty members should not bear the sole responsibility for such an educational campaign; staff members have an essential role to play in this process. I used to have the mistaken impression—shared, I know, by many faculty—that staff members on campus who work in areas like student life or residential life were less focused on the educational mission of the college, and therefore would have little interest in substantive discussions about educational matters on campus. After I became the director of the Honors Program at my college, I found myself working more frequently with staff members from a variety of offices, and I quickly realized how I had misjudged a wide swath of my colleagues. Frequently I find that staff members have a much more direct grasp on the shape and nature of our students' lives than faculty members do; they see them in a wider variety of contexts than we do, and have a better understanding of the many pressures and challenges that our students struggle with on a daily basis. That knowledge could prove extremely valuable in the process of helping students acculturate into the particulars of the academic community. Their formal or informal inclusion in an academic integrity council could also help faculty develop a realistic understanding of what kinds of educational materials and events will hit home with students and what kinds will not.

Finally, we know that one of the main influences on a student's decision to cheat is whether or not he perceives cheating happening around him or believes that his peers approve of cheating. The involvement of student leaders in both the planning and executing of academic honesty materials and events, then, could certainly help reduce a student's impression that his peers approve of cheating. I believe this is one of the reasons that honor code institutions do show lower rates of cheating than noncode institutions—because in honor code institutions students typically play a visible role in formulating and administering the honor policies on campus. For reasons that I have already outlined above, I believe we should not ask students to play the role of honor code police or judges, but we can perhaps gain some of the positive effects of student involvement in an honor code by asking students to contribute to educating their peers about our academic policies. Student leaders, even more so than staff members, can help faculty understand more clearly what their peers find difficult or challenging or unclear about academic honesty policies. Students can also convey to their peers that the academic honesty policies are not a set of arbitrary rules foisted upon the students by the institution. The experiences of former students might prove even more enlightening to current students in this respect. A working journalist who returns to campus to talk about the ways in which properly attributing sources forms an essential part of her work can help students see how the habits of academic honesty they develop at college will continue into their working lives.

Time It Well

We have seen evidence on the importance of timing for helping students make good ethical decisions on a day-by-day basis; clearly, the timing of an educational campaign will also make a huge difference. If we think about the rhythms of both a typical college career and a typical semester, some obvious choices jump out as productive moments of intervention.

Naturally some type of event should occur at the outset of the students' entry into the academic community. The closer that event occurs to the start of the students' first courses, the better. Having them attend an academic honesty education session in June, when they are visiting for a two-day orientation, will likely prove much less effective than having them attend such a session during the days immediately preceding the start of the semester. Of course just such a seminar on academic honesty prior to students taking their first courses is what Ariely described as having little long-term impact on the Princeton students who participated in his experiment. I suspect this may be so for any prematriculation event because it will necessarily be an abstract exercise for the students—they will be learning about how to conduct academically honest work in college before they have had to conduct *any* work in college. We know from lots of learning theory research (including the material we covered in Part II of this book) that people typically learn best by doing—taking concepts or ideas and applying them to real problems and challenges. Lecturing to students about academic honesty, or even having them complete games or exercises or quizzes in order to help them understand what constitutes academically honest work, will not really give students a taste of real problems or challenges.

Still, I would not want college students to come into their first freshman classes without having received any information at all about academic honesty and dishonesty. Tricia Bertram Gallant suggests that one of the problems may be that academic integrity orientations are treated as a small sideshow in the big-tent circus of student life activities. She argues, "Orientations for new students that focus predominantly on student life and extracurricular activities need to be revised to highlight academic culture. It does not mean tagging an honor code–signing ceremony onto the traditional social orientation but fundamentally altering orientation to provide academic socialization. Such a requirement may even require a semester- or year-long freshman seminar."[23] If you don't have the institutional will to implement a full-semester course on academic integrity, a partial solution may be to offer a brief introduction to the topic prior to the first day of classes, perhaps led by faculty and staff, and then to require a follow-up discussion session or exercise of some kind with staff and student leaders within the first few weeks of the semester. In that follow-up—which might be held in the more informal setting of the residence halls—the discussion or exercise leaders could help students analyze the stated academic honesty policies of the syllabi they have received, or have them bring in copies of the first course assignments they have received and consider the potential problems and opportunities those assignments pose for honesty and dishonesty. This would at least give the students some contextual grounding for the lessons on academic honesty to which they had been introduced in the orientation session. Again the goal of such sessions should remain educational. I find that first-semester students in my writing courses typically have some trouble understanding the general expectations of the first assignment I give to them, although they usually don't even know enough to realize what they don't understand and ask questions; having upperclass student leaders work with first-year students both to understand the expectations of the assignment and to consider what honest and dishonest responses to it might look like would prove a welcome development for many of my students.

Beyond those opening weeks of intervention, the rhythms of the semester will vary for each student, since not every class will offer its midterms at the same time, and every student will have different times during the semester when she is most pressured by her academic work. I think the simple solution here might be for staff and student leaders to work together to orchestrate both paper and electronic campaigns that provide regular reminders to students about their obligations to academic honesty. A great grounded assessment for a graphic design class on campus might be to develop printed materials on academic honesty, such as flyers and posters, that can be placed in residence halls and classrooms and common areas. You can find plenty of beautiful model posters, from the University of Windsor, at the website for the International Center for Academic Integrity.[24] On my campus we also receive an email digest every day with a list of the day's campus events as well as with reminders about upcoming deadlines and other announcements. It would not be too difficult to place reminders about academic honesty within these messages during the middle of the semester, when students are most likely to be inundated with midterms, and especially at the end of the semester, as they are preparing final papers and projects and studying for final exams.

The keys to success in any such campaign, whether it takes place on paper or electronically or both, would be to ensure that it happens with creativity and probably humor, and that it does not become such a constant presence in students' lives that it turns into white noise the students can tune out. For both of these reasons I think the participation of student leaders would be essential, since they can help evaluate what will have the greatest impact on students and can provide feedback on how much campaigning might prove to be too much.

Focus Academic Integrity Campaigns on Education, Not Ethics

Unless you are an ethics professor, you are not an ethics professor. You are, however, in the business of education—whether you are a faculty member, a staff member, or a former faculty member working in administration. For this reason, I believe that the focus of any academic honesty training for students—whether it's conducted by your staff at freshman orientation or by faculty members in the classroom—should remain squarely upon educating students about what academic honesty means, and should *not* attempt to harangue them into behaving in ethical ways. Perhaps there are other situations in which you might want to harangue your students into behaving in ethical ways —at the Catholic college where I teach, for example, college ceremonies are frequently overlaid with religious language and themes that quite explicitly address their ethics and character formation, and I think that's perfectly wonderful. But I don't believe that's what we should be doing when we are educating students about academic honesty.

As we saw above, Dan Ariely and his colleagues demonstrated that the Princeton University crash course on academic honesty and ethics did little to influence the behavior of students on his standard cheating-inducing math test. We can see additional evidence of how academic ethics training fails to influence behavior in a study conducted by Donald McCabe and two colleagues that appeared in a 1994 issue of the *Journal of Business Ethics*. In their study, McCabe and his colleagues administered surveys to more than 800 incoming graduate students in MBA programs and law school. The surveys asked questions about the students' values and had them "respond to selected ethical decision making vignettes."[25] The researchers then returned to a smaller sampling of those same students and gave them a similar survey in the semester just prior to their degree completion. The business students showed a slight but insignificant improvement in their approach to resolving the problems posed by the vignettes; the law students showed a small and significant improvement. But then the researchers compared the results of students in both programs who had taken an optional ethics course with students who had not. The result? No differences at all. "We are forced to conclude," they write, "that the ethics course did not have any significant impact on students' value profiles or their resolution of ethical dilemmas."[26] We might think again here of the problem of transfer, and of the possibility that the ethics training that the students received in their courses was confined to the courses they took and did not travel with them to the surveys they completed—or, more disturbingly, to the world outside of their graduate program.[27]

So focus your academic integrity campaign on the education. When students step onto campus for the first time, they are entering a community that has its own unique set of ethical standards and behavior codes. Although our incoming students may have received some education about those standards in high school, we should assume that they have not, and that they need explicit education in terms of how they should conduct their academic work in the ways that we expect. The particular focus of such educational campaigns should remain as much as possible on helping students understand how to incorporate ethically the writings, ideas, and images of other human beings into their own work. Students probably do not need much help in understanding that they should not peer at the exam of the person sitting next to them, or that they should not purchase essays from term paper mills. But, as many writers in this area have correctly pointed out, they do need help in understanding the standards that we have for distinguishing between their own work and the work they have appropriated from others. As Susan Blum has argued, the standards that we expect students to follow in these areas may strike them as both foreign and nonsensical: "The official rules governing citation, stemming from Enlightenment notions of authorship, ownership, and originality, and the distinction between ideas and expression of ideas, are simply not accepted by today's college students. They quote constantly in their ordinary lives and rarely have to cite their sources."[28] Hence we should focus our education in academic honesty first on helping students understand the distinction between what Blum calls "student citation norms" and "academic citation norms," second on helping them understand how to adhere to the latter type of norms, and third on the consequences that will attend to not doing so. (I discuss what consequences should look like in Chapter 11.)

If you teach for long enough—and probably it won't take more than a few semesters—you are bound to have an encounter with a cheating student in which the student pleads guilty by way of ignorance: "I didn't know we weren't allowed to do that." Sometimes that excuse will be a last-ditch attempt to escape punishment, but sometimes it will be legitimate. Some students really do not understand the way we do things around here, or they might have an abstract awareness of academic norms but don't realize that we consider them to be important, and that we really do expect them to follow those norms. As one British writer wittily described this problem, for some students the "perceived complexity associated with understanding plagiarism is not unlike the 'off side' rule in football, that is, it is obvious to the enthusiast but a complete mystery to the outsider and there exist many degrees of understanding between these extremes."[29] A well-established educational campaign on the norms of academic honesty should help students learn the rules of our game.

A really effective educational campaign will not only teach students the mechanics of citing their sources properly in an academic context, but will help them understand *why* they should do so. It will help them understand what we mean when we ask them for "original work" on their homework assignments or essays, and why we ask them for it, and why we allow or don't allow collaboration on individual assignments. I would argue that specific conversations about the "why's" of academic integrity belong in our classrooms, since the shape of such conversations will vary according to the expectations of each discipline and faculty member. And I suspect that such discussions will have more impact in our classrooms, where students are more attuned to learning, than they will at some general orientation session. Before we can offer explanations on the "why's" of academic integrity to our students, though, we have to be clear on them ourselves—and, as I will argue in the next chapter, that may be a more complicated matter than you might expect.

9

ON ORIGINAL WORK

Despite the many common objectives we have as teachers in higher education—such as the goal of teaching our students to write well—we all know that each of our disciplines has its own standards for thinking and writing and conducting scholarly work. If a student in my Creative Nonfiction course handed me a paper that was written in the passive-voiced prose typical of a piece of research in the sciences or social sciences, I would mark it all up and send it back for revision. A student in my Senior Seminar who turned in a research paper using APA formatting and citation would get the same treatment. To a certain extent, we can see similar distinctions between what defines academically honest and dishonest work within the disciplines. When I am asking students to write their original interpretations of works of literature we are studying, I assume that they will derive those interpretations on their own, without collaborating with their peers. Joe Hoyle, by contrast, expects and encourages his students to get together before class and discuss the questions and problems in his course, perhaps because he well knows how collaboration will play an important role in their careers as accountants.

No doubt many (if not most) of the standards of academic honesty are shared ones—shared among Joe Hoyle in accounting, you in chemistry, me in English, and the students in all three of our courses. We all know that you don't peer at your neighbor's exam and copy down the answers you see there, that you don't cut and paste material from the internet without citing it, and that you don't hire someone else to write a paper or take a test for you. In response to a question about the difference between healthy and unhealthy foods, a diet guru I saw on public television late one night pointed out that if he loaded up a table with a bunch of healthy and unhealthy foods, a six-year-old would probably give you a pretty accurate estimation of which foods fell into which categories. The same is true of academic honesty across the disciplines: most of the behaviors we think about as academically dishonest would be dishonest in any class on campus, and would be recognized as such by your students. So I am not suggesting that we need to offer discipline-specific education to our students on how not to cheat on exams, or how not to plagiarize from Wikipedia. They know that stuff already.

Where matters become more complicated is in the fuzzy territory of what we mean when we ask our students, either individually or in collaboration, to produce "original" work—as I typically ask my students to do when they are writing interpretations of the works of literature we are studying, and as I suspect many of us do when we give out-of-class assessments (and even in-class assessments). "I don't want to hear what some hack writer for SparkNotes thinks about 'Goblin Market,'" I will say to them. "I want to hear what *you* think about it. So give me your own, original interpretation of the poem using the readings from class and the ideas we generated in our course discussion."

To which injunction I am quite certain many students might respond with two very pointed questions: First, "*How* on earth can I, a junior English major, be expected to come up with an original reading of such a complex poem when literary scholars with advanced degrees have been plumbing its depths for more than a hundred years?" And second, "*Why* on earth do you want me to come up with an "original" interpretation of the poem when a hundred years of study have likely produced dozens of interpretations much better than mine?"

Phrased more generally, I think these two questions are ones that students might pose to faculty in any discipline: *how* do I produce my own work in this discipline, and *why* does it matter that I produce my own work? Those two general questions, it seems to me, are ones that each discipline—and perhaps even each faculty member and each course—has to answer distinctively. And those two questions, it also seems to me, can help form the basis for the more substantial conversation you have with your students about academic honesty and dishonesty in your courses, in addition to the general conversations they might be having through educational campaigns on campus. I can't answer those two questions for you, since I don't know what expectations an engineer or a scientist or a linguist or a psychologist might have for students to produce their own original work in those disciplines. So rather than trying to produce a laundry list of what academic honesty looks like in each discipline, and why we expect it of our students, I am simply going to walk through an analysis of what I mean when I ask my students for original work, and why I want them to do it. Afterward, we will consider what aspects of my answers to those two questions belong in my conversations with students. Like any good English professor, I prefer my lessons to come in the form of stories, so I will begin my answer to the two questions of my skeptical (and hypothetical) student above with a (real) tale of one student and two assignments.

Every year on or around January 25th, lovers of Scotland's most famous bard, Robert Burns, celebrate the anniversary of his birth in 1759 with a traditional evening of poetry, music, drink, and food. Burns Suppers, as they are known, might include readings of some of Burns's poems, a dinner of traditional Scottish foods such as haggis or neeps and tatties (turnips and potatoes), performances of folk songs composed or collected by Burns, and plenty of ceremonial toasting and drinking of various forms of whiskey. At a pub near my home that hosts a Burns Supper every year, the evening kicks off with a bagpiper. The Burns Supper helps unite Scots at home and abroad, and lovers of all things Scottish, in a commemoration of the man who still stirs the national pride.

Not a Scot by birthland or ethnic heritage, I have nevertheless long been a lover of the poetry of Robert Burns. So when the opportunity came around for my turn to teach the British Literature Survey II course a couple of years ago (which covers literature from Great Britain and Ireland from the end of the eighteenth century to the present day), I naturally gravitated toward Robert Burns as the starting point for the semester. And when I immersed myself in Burns's work while I was preparing for the course, I decided that we would end the semester with a traditional Burns Supper in which students in the course would offer performances or readings of the authors we had read in the course in the same way that Burns Supper participants celebrate the works of the famous bard. Then I quickly noted that I could not toast with or drink whiskey with my students, that I didn't know any bagpipers, that I did not really want to prepare neeps and tatties for thirty students, and that the students would probably rather eat pages from their anthology than a plateful of haggis. So I scaled back my original plans somewhat, but still held onto the notion that we would finish the semester with an evening event in which groups of students would select an author or set of authors that we had read, put together some kind of performance or presentation on that person's work and its continuing relevance for our lives today, and have some tea and desserts. Ah, as Burns would say, the best-laid schemes . . .

I called the event Burns and Beyond (to indicate that students could present on authors other than Burns) and have held it for the past two years I have taught the course. I count it as one of the most enjoyable evenings of the year, and the student evaluations tell me that the students enjoy it as well. Some students embrace the opportunity to engage in really creative endeavors—such as performing scenes from works we have read, or joining me in musical performances of songs by Burns—while others tend toward more traditional presentations. Nonetheless, they all do an excellent job of fulfilling the main purpose of the assignment: identifying and tracing out connections between the British literature we have read and contemporary cultural productions or political issues from their worlds today. Students have linked poems and stories and plays to obscure American television shows, to songs by rap and country musicians, to debates about the environment, and to popular films. Although I try to ensure that they do not simply collapse important differences between the past and the present, I do want them to see that the works of the writers we have read can still speak to us and help us think more deeply about the cultural and political issues that confront us today.[1]

In my second Burns and Beyond event, one of the best presentations came from a group of students who were English majors with concentrations in elementary or secondary education. The four women in this group decided to take a short story that we had read in class, James Joyce's "Eveline," and put together a lesson plan that could be used to teach this story to middle school students. They drew their inspiration for this from the methods courses they had taken in their education concentration, where they had learned how to construct such plans according to the state's curricular frameworks and objectives. During their presentation they reviewed the lesson plan in detail, which included comparing the story to a painting by one of their friends that sounded one of the same themes explored in "Eveline." They also showed us the ways in which their lesson plan matched up with the various aspects of the state curriculum framework, interspersing quotations from those guidelines throughout their PowerPoint presentation. The presentation was one of the best ones I have seen in the course of two years of running this event, and they earned themselves a well-deserved A.

What made this all the more surprising and gratifying to me was the fact that one of the members of this group, whom we will call Mary, had been a student in my class three semesters prior to that one, and had cheated on the first assignment of the semester. That class was the gateway course for English majors, in which we run all new majors through a gauntlet of challenging assignments designed to prepare them to write and think effectively in their upper-level courses. In the first assignment of the semester, students were required to write a summary of the main argument of the first chapter of the textbook, on New Critical literary interpretation, and then apply that argument to a poem we had read. When I read Mary's paper, some of the sentences struck me as immediately familiar. After puzzling over them for a few minutes, I looked at the textbook chapter and saw that she had plagiarized those familiar sentences from the textbook. *Really?* I called her in, went through the standard procedures with her (about which I will say more in the next chapter), and we moved forward from there. She seemed genuinely chastised by the incident and became one of the hardest-working students in the class that semester. Even if I had never had her in class again, I would have counted her turnaround in that class as a success story; to see her play a role in the outstanding presentation by her group at the Burns and Beyond celebration made the whole story a doubly satisfying one for me.

But let's pause here to think about the difference between the two assignments she completed. In the presentation that she did with her group, the students relied essentially on the interpretation of "Eveline" that we put together in our class discussion of the story. They did not offer a revolutionary reading of Joyce's narrative techniques; it was a fairly conventional reading, citing some of the passages that I had highlighted and analyzed for them in our discussion. They relied on what they had learned in their education courses to construct the main framework for their presentation, and included quoted material from the state's curriculum frameworks. They put into the presentation a painting done by one of their friends, a student who was not in our course. In that sense, you might argue, very little of what the students presented to us could be considered as their own, original work. The same, of course, was true of the summary that Mary wrote for me in the gateway course; she was punished in that course, however, for not producing her own, original work.

Suppose an observer from outside our educational system pointed out to me that in both cases Mary relied on the work of other people to complete her assignment—but in one case was punished for it, and in another case rewarded for it. I could easily point out in response that one major distinction between the two cases was that, in the first instance, Mary did not provide proper credit for the work she had cited from the textbook; in the second instance, she and her groupmates did provide that credit for each of the works they cited. Suppose that observer were to push me a little further on this, however, and ask whether that one little fact—whether or not she named her source—was really all that made the difference between a failed assignment and an excellent one. To that objection I might respond that, no, even if Mary had put quotes around all of the material she had plagiarized from the textbook in the first assignment, that would not have been enough to earn her an A on that summary. What earned Mary and her classmates an A on the later presentation was their ability to create new and interesting connections within a disparate set of materials that they pulled from multiple sources. This, I would argue, is what we actually refer to—at least in my discipline—when we talk about "original" or "creative" or "innovative" thinking. What Mary did in her summary assignment was simply repeat the words of someone else without making any substantial connections between those words and anything meaningful that she already knew or was able to discover from the assignment. And this, I would argue, is what we usually label as "rote" or "uninspired" or "unoriginal"—and even sometimes "dishonest"—thinking.

Suppose my hypothetical interlocutor (or skeptical student) were to push me even further now, reminding me that—like many of my colleagues—I frequently admonish students that I don't want them simply to repeat what I have told them, or what they have read in their textbooks, or what they read on SparkNotes or from other online sources. I tell them instead that I want them to give me their own "original" thinking on the works of literature we are studying in class. Do I really expect them to come up with "original" interpretations of a story like "Eveline," which has been pored over and analyzed by Joyce scholars and literature students for close to a hundred years now, and which would hardly seem to lend itself to original thinking by anyone these days? Of course I don't. In fact, what I really expect, although I do not always articulate this to them, is precisely what Mary and her group did in our Burns and Beyond presentation: take the material from the course and construct original *connections* between that material and other material from my course and previous courses. In the case of my presentations, which encouraged them to build connections to productions or issues outside of the course, the students did precisely that. But not all courses or assignments, including my own, come with that expectation. Sometimes we simply expect students to make connections between what we taught them yesterday and what we are teaching today, or what will come tomorrow. Sometimes we expect connections between what they are learning in this course in their major and what they learned in the last course in their major. Sometimes we expect connections between the last assignment and the next one, between what we said at the beginning of class and what we say at the end, or between concept A and concept B.

So it turns out that when I tell my students I want them to express their own, original interpretations of the works of literature we are studying in class, instead of copying the interpretations they find on SparkNotes, with or without giving that source the proper credit, I don't actually expect them to develop "original" interpretations of works of literature that have been under the microscope for decades or even centuries—at least if you take "original" to mean "never been thought of or published by anyone in human history before." I expect them instead to create an original *network of connections,* using the different features of the work, the work and the author's biography, the historical contextual material to which I have introduced them, the critical approaches we have studied in class, their own personal experiences, and any other potential texts or ideas that they believe might help create a richer interpretive network. And if my observer were to push me even further and ask me why I want my students to do *that,* I might respond that, whenever we are talking about original or innovative or creative thinking, we are usually talking about precisely this: connecting in new ways with pre-existing concepts or facts or theories, and using these connections to experience productive new ways of thinking or acting or feeling. That's what the creation of knowledge usually means—the creation of new connections among pre-existing data or theories, which sometimes helps form new data or theories. The digital age has helped us see this more clearly, since we are all more and more aware of the fact that the amount of pre-existing knowledge in the world is staggeringly large. We don't expect our students or even ourselves to create knowledge *ex nihilo;* we expect instead, to quote E. M. Forster, to "only connect."

If my questioner (who would by now be starting to annoy me) were to push me just one step further and ask me why I want my students to engage in the process of building such connections, as opposed to leaving that work to the advanced scholars in my field, I would point to the literature on human learning to suggest that such connection-building exercises do not merely help us push knowledge in new directions, but also help students learn what we are teaching them more deeply. As Susan Ambrose and her colleagues point out, one main difference between experts and novices in any given field will be "the number or density of connections among the concepts, facts, and skills they know."[2] So novice learners will tend to have facts or skills learned in isolation from one another, and separate from other things they have learned. Experts in a field, by contrast, have rich networks of connections among the various pieces of knowledge they have, and are able to absorb new knowledge by situating it within those richly developed contexts, associating it with other facts or theories. So by asking my students to engage in activities in which they are building their "original" interpretations of a work of literature by creating a unique set of connections within a work, between that work and other works we have studied in the course, and between the work and elements they have studied outside the course, I am helping them to build richer knowledge networks around my course material, which leads to and reflects deeper learning of that material. Because she now associates the story "Eveline" with material from her education courses, with a painting by a friend, and with my course, "Mary" will likely remember and reflect upon that story much more frequently than she will on the theory of New Critical literary interpretation, which she was learning only for the sake of one assignment.

And so we have arrived once again at that happy juncture where more learning and less cheating meet and join hands. Students who have the opportunity to create their own "original" networks of connections between our course material and their previous or current knowledge learn the material more deeply than students who simply encounter and copy the networks established by others, whether that "copying" takes the form of authorized summaries of some great thinker or unauthorized reproductions of something they found on the internet. Hearkening back to one of the guides we considered in the chapter on intrinsic motivation, we can see how Andy Kaufman's students, for example, are compelled to create unique or original connections between the works of Russian literature they are studying and the human beings sitting in front of them in the juvenile detention center. So Kaufman's journaling assignments not only eliminate any possibility for the students to cheat in that course—since they depend on the students' specific experience with the juvenile offenders—*and* foster intrinsic motivation, but they also help the students create richer connections between the literature they are reading and the world around them, thus leading them (according to the theory of connected knowledge) to learn it more deeply.

This theorizing about the connection between originality and learning came about as a result of confronting and thinking hard about a very legitimate question that our students might pose to us: in the digital age, *how* and *why* do we expect them to come up with their own ideas and create their own work instead of simply relying on the vast amount of ideas that exist out there already? We expect them to come up with their own ideas about our course material because it helps them learn it more deeply, and we expect them to do so by building connections between our course material and other material they have learned or are learning. As the example of both my Burns and Beyond students and Andy Kaufman's students might suggest, I think the more we can push them to create connections that stretch outside of the boundaries of our specific classrooms, and even outside the boundaries of our disciplines or our campus, the more likely they are to build up the kind of really rich and interesting networks of connections that might inspire new knowledge and create learning that will last a lifetime.

That's a statement that I am willing to make only from my limited perspective as a teacher of literature. It may be, after all, that the expectations of a professor in engineering or chemistry or accountancy do not quite look like this. And so I think the two questions with which we started this section are ones that have to be answered by every faculty member individually:

> *What* does it mean for students to do their own work in my discipline?
> *Why* does it matter?

It may be that many of our answers will look the same, just as many of our expectations for good writing—such as clarity and organization—will look the same. But we won't know that until and unless we begin to think more explicitly about these questions and talk about how the answers to them manifest in each of our disciplines. First and foremost, I think those conversations are ones that we should hold with each other, in order to clarify the answers for ourselves. Once we have worked out our answers, we can then determine how much of this belongs in the conversations we have with our students about cheating.

Here again, I think that decisions about that can and will vary according to both discipline and individual faculty temperament. I tend to favor transparency in all things in my teaching; I am constantly explaining to my students the reasons behind whatever we are doing or whatever I am asking them to do. I suspect that students sometimes are looking at me and thinking, "Just teach, dude; quit explaining everything." So I do hold conversations with my students in which I encourage them to draw in texts or theories from other classes they are taking, and I talk to them about how learning works, and I tell them why I tend to run class by discussion rather than lecturing. But that probably reflects my personality more than anything else—as my wife will happily tell you, I can't keep a secret to save my life, and I've written many hundreds of pages about my personal life in my books and essays. You may work and teach differently, and feel less compelled to review with your students the educational philosophies that animate your academic honesty policies.

But I would argue that, in the face of the continuous changes we are seeing both to the nature of information and to the shape of higher education, we are all compelled to ask ourselves these questions and formulate our own answers—and we are equally compelled to make the reasoning behind our academic integrity policies at least available to students, if not to speak with them directly about it. In Ken Bain's *What the Best College Teachers Do,* he cites the work of Donald Saari, a math professor from the University of California, who gives his students free rein, at any point in the course, to ask him "Who Gives a Damn?" about whatever they are doing in the course that day. In response to that question, Bain says, Saari will always "stop and explain to the students why the material under consideration at that moment—however abstruse and minuscule a piece of the big picture it may be—is important, and how it relates to the larger questions and issues of the course."[3] Likewise I think we have to remain open to the skeptical students who might ask "Why bother?" Why should they bother to memorize or learn or connect or do their own work when technology can often provide them with the information they need (more) quickly and efficiently? Why should they bother to do their own work when others can do it better and more easily? Why should they bother to complete an assignment on their own when three of them working together may complete it more effectively?

Those are good questions, deserving of answers—first to ourselves, as fully as possible, and then to our students, in whatever form you believe will help them make a deeper and stronger commitment to academic honesty.

10

RESPONDING TO CHEATING

As much as I would love to direct the entire focus of this book toward educational approaches to cheating, part of any institution's approach to academic integrity has to address the most effective means of responding to a cheating student. If your goal is to curb cheating on campus—as of course it should be—the first type of response that might come to mind would be to impose harsh penalties on offenders. Many honor code institutions, for example, use a severe and uniformly applied punishment, such as failure of the course, for all academic honesty violations, first offenses included. The reasoning behind such hard punishment seems to be that students are well informed about the consequences of cheating from the moment they step onto an honor code campus and receive frequent reminders about those consequences, and so have no one to blame but themselves for their violations. We might also be tempted to apply such hard uniform punishments as a mode of deterring students from cheating in the first place—raise the stakes on the consequences, and you may lower the willingness of students to hazard an encounter with those consequences. Surely, you might think, students will cheat less on a campus where first offenders receive an automatic one-semester suspension from the university than they will from an institution that has a more staggered and negotiable system of punishments.

Believe what you will, but the evidence from cheating surveys does not consistently support the notion that hard punishments deter potential cheaters. Donald McCabe and one of his co-researchers, Linda Klebe Trevino, hypothesized in a 1997 article in the journal *Research in Higher Education* that a survey of close to two thousand students on multiple campuses would reveal that cheating rates were lower at institutions where students perceived the penalties for academic dishonesty as most severe. The results of the survey, to their surprise, did not support that hypothesis: "Perceived severity of penalties for cheating was significant . . . but the direction of the relationship was opposite of that predicted. Cheating was higher for students who perceived that the penalties for cheating at their school were more severe."[1] Could this finding be just some strange anomaly? If so, it's a recurring one. McCabe and his various co-authors reported on the same relationship between perceived severity of penalties and cheating rates in at least four different articles. In their cross-cultural comparison of cheating rates in the United States and Lebanon, McCabe and his co-authors theorize that this recurring finding may be the result of a statistical quirk called the "suppression effect."[2] Whatever the reason, the finding has surfaced in multiple surveys that cheating rates are actually higher at institutions where students perceive the penalties for academic dishonesty to be most severe.

To be fair, that's not the whole story. Other researchers have used different methods to try and establish the link you might expect between cheating rates and penalty severity. The researchers at Midwestern State University, who compared cheating rates over a twenty-year period, including after the addition of their honor code, also asked students about three potential categories of deterrents to cheating—social disapproval, guilt, and punishments—asking them to rate the effectiveness of each category. "Punitive deterrents," they found, "were rated as more effective than either social deterrents or guilt by both cheaters and noncheaters."[3] The authors conclude from this that "a credible threat of punishment appears to be the best deterrent to academic dishonesty."[4] I am not as convinced of this conclusion as the authors seem to be. They base this recommendation on what students told them, in an anonymous survey, about what the most effective deterrents to cheating *might be*—not on the deterrent strategies at their institutions. I suspect that students might have answered this question just as anyone might have, student or no: if you want to deter cheaters, give harsh punishments. Political and social theorists have been using this deterrent argument for a long time now to justify the death penalty. But as anyone knows who wades into the literature on the deterrent impact of the death penalty, what seems obvious to us turns out be almost impossible to verify through empirical research. So I would suggest the possibility that perhaps students were simply applying that same logic—harsh penalties deter crimes— to the survey question about effective deterrents to cheating, and hence that we should not draw any firm conclusions from it about punishments as deterrent.

I don't want to argue too vehemently with the conclusion of these researchers, because all I really want to suggest here is that, when it comes to the question of whether or not severe punishments deter cheating, the waters are muddy. We can see that from McCabe's surveys, and we can see it, I believe, even in surveys that might, on the surface, seem to support the notion that harsh penalties deter cheating. So the only conclusion I want to draw from that research is the following: *we have no incontrovertible evidence that harsh penalties deter cheating.* Some surveys seem to suggest that they might, and some actually suggest the possibility that cheating happens more frequently on campuses with harsh penalties. So with that in mind, I would argue that we should not construct campuswide policies on cheating based on the notion that extremely severe penalties will deter it; we simply do not have the evidence to support that idea, no matter how intuitively logical it might seem.

If we take that factor out of the equation, we might ask ourselves what other reasons we could adduce in order to justify severe, uniform punishments for all academic honesty offenses. One understandable (but not very good) reason for campuses to institute such a system would be that it simplifies the "penalty phase" of cheating cases. If you're guilty, you receive the one and only available punishment. No deliberating about intention, or degrees of honesty, and so on. The dean at a small college I visited to discuss their cheating policies told me that the campus had tried to modify their honor code in order to allow more flexibility in their responses to cheating, but had quickly abandoned the attempt when it became clear how much more complicated it made the process. "I came to think about cheating more like pregnancy," the dean said to me. "You can't be partly pregnant; you're either completely pregnant or not pregnant at all. And that's how we handle cheating around here." Putting this strange analogy aside, where I think it belongs, I would argue that it makes much more sense to think about our responses to cheating in the way that we respond to crimes in our legal system: we take the time to consider the nature and degree of the offense, and we give out an appropriate punishment. We do not give the same punishment to petty thieves and murderers. When it comes to academic honesty, I think we should be able to make at least some of the same distinctions as we do in our legal system.

But that analogy does not quite work either, because the legal system has the simple responsibility of maintaining order in our society, whereas those of us on college campuses have the responsibility of helping human beings learn. And so I believe the best reason we have for *not* instituting hard and uniform punishments for first-time offenders, especially the punishment that you will find in many honor code institutions (that is, failure of the course), is that such responses do a terrible job of helping students learn. Quite obviously, a student who automatically fails a course is removed from any further potential learning experiences he might have had in the course. A student who automatically fails an assignment on which he has cheated, and which he has no chance to redo, also fails to learn anything from that assignment. So harsh and uniform punishments will put an automatic stop to the learning that the course was designed to instill in the students. It may be that a severe penalty for a first infraction helps a student learn an important lesson about academic honesty—namely, that the school sees it as vitally important, since it tolerates no violations of it. But it may also be that the students are learning other lessons from such a punishment at the same time: that the institution values rules over learning, or that it affords students no second chances, or that the institution's faculty operate as if they were on a battlefield, hell-bent on catching and punishing cheaters, instead of providing a learning environment in which all constituents are working together to help students learn.

I would add, as a final argument against harsh and uniform punishments, that such punishments are one very likely reason for students' reluctance to report perceived violations to their teachers or administrators. Put yourself in the position of a student who has observed an acquaintance using a cheat sheet on an exam. You don't know this student very well and feel no special loyalty or sense of obligation to her. But you do know that if you contribute evidence to a charge of academic dishonesty brought against that student, she will fail the course. Failing a course can have major repercussions on a student's life. It might cause athletes to lose their eligibility, merit scholars to lose their awards, and weaker students to be put on academic probation or expelled. As an eighteen-year-old student, how willing would you be to help create those kinds of consequences for another student at your institution? Now put yourself in the position of a student who knows that first offenders are offered a second chance, and that the student will only receive a severe punishment if what you observed was the result of a second or third documented offense, and hence likely the actions of a serially dishonest student. How much more willing would you be to report what you have seen under those circumstances, or at least provide corroborating testimony in an investigation? Although I can't point to any evidence to support this supposition, it would not surprise me at all to learn that peer reporting rates were actually *lower* at honor code institutions, with their typically harsh and uniform punishments, than they are at noncode institutions, despite the fact that not reporting a witnessed violation constitutes a violation of the code.

So this leads us toward a more moderate response. I would argue that an effective cheating policy which maintains education as its focus should allow for some flexibility in the application of penalties, and that faculty members are the ones who will know best how to help a student learn from a cheating violation in their own courses. But I would also argue that the campus as a whole must maintain vigilance in preventing repeat offenses and in conveying to students the seriousness of academic integrity on campus. With this wish list in mind, I will offer one very modest proposal for what a campus policy on cheating might look like. Parts of this policy are modeled on the one in use at my institution; parts of it come from my own thinking about the topic; and parts of it come from policies I have seen at other institutions. I will present the basic response strategy first, and then enumerate the four basic principles that underpin this proposal. The proposal could certainly be used to formulate alternative policies, or it could be modified to suit other types of learning environment.

A Basic Response Strategy to Cheating

When a faculty member suspects a student of cheating, she confronts the student with the allegation and with two possible courses of action.

1. If the student chooses to deny the charge, his case is automatically referred to an academic honesty board, which consists of a mixed body of administrators, faculty, and students.[5] That board has the responsibility of investigating the violation, making a judgment, and, if necessary, administering an appropriate punishment.

2. If the student chooses to acknowledge the violation, she is presented with a "settlement" form which states in detail a punishment that the faculty member for the course has proposed for the violation. This punishment can be anything from redoing the assignment for full credit to failing the course altogether. The decision for this punishment lies entirely within the hands of the faculty member. By signing this form, the student acknowledges her guilt and accepts the punishment; the faculty member signs the form as well, and in doing so agrees that the punishment is the only one the student will receive for the violation in the course. Settlement forms are placed in the student's file in a central office on campus and remain there until at least one year after graduation.

Any student who signs the settlement form or is found guilty of a cheating violation must also complete an academic integrity educational experience of some kind. That might take the form of a short course that the institution offers each semester, or it might take the form of a half-day workshop, or it might consist of a specific assignment or set of assignments the student must complete. There may be one experience for plagiarists and another for those who fabricate lab data, or it may be the same for all students. The campus officer who handles academic integrity violations could work together with a faculty team to devise these educational experiences.

A student who has a signed confession form in his file and who faces a second cheating allegation must face the academic honesty board. I believe that this could justifiably be the place to implement a hard and uniform penalty, if institutions are so inclined. For example, all repeat violators would automatically fail the course or be expelled or suspended from the institution for a semester. A student who has signed the settlement form and taken a short course on cheating and then repeats the violation strikes me as someone who may not be ready for college, and who might benefit from some time away from the course or the institution.

The use of this system, which of course can be modified in a variety of ways, accomplishes the four objectives that I believe should animate any campuswide response policy.

1. *The response is consistent with the seriousness of the offense.* My institution uses a version of the settlement form described above. Despite the fact that the signing of this form may levy absolutely no additional punishment on students, I can assure you from experience that students are horrified at the prospect of a signed confession of academic dishonesty being lodged in their file in the dean's office. When Mary, the student who cheated in my gateway course in her sophomore year, came into my office to sign the settlement form, she was deeply and visibly shaken. I have little doubt that her signing that form made a serious impact on her perceptions of the seriousness of her offense. I have never caught a student cheating and found that it was a second offense, which means that—if my experience is representative, which may or may

not be the case—we are mostly catching first offenders, who are then staying on the straight and narrow for the rest of their time in college. I suspect that punishments for cheating remain very abstract and theoretical in a student's mind until they are experienced. Signing the form, along with a clear understanding of what will follow a second violation, does an excellent job of scaring students straight.

2. *The response allows for discrimination in applying penalties to both first-time and repeat offenders.* The penalty decision for first-time offenders remains in the hands of the faculty member, where I think it belongs. This gives faculty the leeway they need in order to impose a penalty that fits the course and the student, and which will ensure that the student stays on track in terms of his learning in the course. Some faculty may choose to impose a default penalty of a failing grade on the exam or assignment, but others might choose more creative penalties that drive home the lessons of academic honesty. More power to them. For a repeat offender, I would argue that the penalties should be much more severe, since a second offense after signing the settlement form suggests that the student clearly did not absorb the lesson the first time around. Failure of the course or a full-semester suspension seems like an appropriate response to such an offense, and some institutions may choose to mandate such penalties for all second offenses; but of course others might choose to allow their academic honesty board to retain the power to impose lighter or different sentences.

3. *The responses contribute to the student's learning.* This can happen in two ways. Since first-time offenders will typically remain in the course in which they cheated, the faculty member has the opportunity to ensure students return to that course material they were trying to cheat their way around and learn it correctly. The faculty member also has the oppor-

tunity to impose additional assignments or penalties, which might help the students learn about the importance of academic integrity in their course or their discipline.[6] But the educational experience required of all cheating students gives the institution a final opportunity to ensure that the student learns from the experience and comes away from it with a better understanding of both academic integrity and its vital role in an educational environment.

4. *The response reduces bureaucracy.* The best practical argument for this response system may be that, faced with the choice between the low consequences of signing the form and the potentially high consequences of fighting the charge, most guilty students will sign the form, reducing the number of cases that must be dealt with by faculty and the academic honesty board. As Tricia Bertram Gallant has pointed out, "the efforts to police misconduct, follow institutional policies, and prove academic misconduct in evidentiary hearings place additional burdens on faculty that are not only unacknowledged and unrewarded but also emotionally draining."[7] A good academic integrity response policy should acknowledge this reality by streamlining the process as much as possible without compromising the rights of the accused. Students will be most likely to shortcut the full board hearing and accept the settlement form process if faculty members impose light penalties for first offenses or simply ask students to redo the test or assignment without penalty.[8]

The use of a settlement form and an educational experience for first offenders, to be followed by more severe and uniform sanctions for repeaters, seems to me to fulfill all of the major objectives for a response system that is focused on learning and that reduces the burden on faculty and administrators. But it certainly does not represent the only way to accomplish those objectives. And I will be the first to acknowledge that the settlement form system has a fatal flaw: it will achieve the desired objectives *only if all faculty comply*. If faculty are striking private deals with students for academic honesty violations, then students can continue to cheat in class after class without serious consequences. If you want to reduce cheating on the campus as a whole, then the campus as a whole has to work together not only in educating students about academic honesty but in responding to it when it occurs. So before I can conclude this final section of the book, we have to take a few pages to consider how individual faculty members should align their courses to the campus academic integrity policies, whether they take the form described above or any other.

11

CHEATING IN YOUR CLASSROOM

Let's assume for the moment that you have followed all of the (excellent) advice given in this book. You have restructured your courses in ways designed to increase learning and reduce cheating, and you have convinced your colleagues and your campus to undertake an academic honesty education initiative and modify their response policy following the guidelines outlined in the previous chapters. You have done absolutely everything in your power to reduce the incentive and opportunity for students to cheat in your courses and on campus. Will you still have students cheating in your courses? Of course. You are always going to have students who are in college because their parents want them to be there and who won't care about your course material no matter inspiring you may be, or students who fall desperately behind in the wake of some personal tragedy and can't see any other way out, or students who are just poorly developed human beings and who see nothing wrong with cheating. In the face of that hard reality, the final strategies we need to consider are the ones that involve handling cheating incidents in your courses, and ensuring that your responses align with your institutional policies. The three main pressure points at which you have to ensure such alignment occur in the statement of your own policies, the moment of confrontation with a cheating student, and your individual response to that student.

Speaking about Cheating

I don't particularly enjoy speaking to my own students about cheating. I think my discomfort at holding that conversation with my students, in any form, comes from wishful thinking or perhaps willful ignorance: if neither I nor my students speak about cheating, then maybe it really isn't happening. But if we do not speak about cheating with our students, despite the fact that some students are cheating (and we know they are), we are sending to the students one (or both) of the following messages: "I'm too stupid to realize that cheating is happening in my courses"; or "I don't really care that cheating is happening in my courses." I would suggest gently that neither of those messages are ones that we want to convey to our students. You might rightly be wondering, though, what remains for you to say to your students about cheating if, as we both hope will be the case, they are receiving a thorough education in academic honesty and dishonesty from their orientation program and the subsequent follow-up initiatives that your campus has developed.

In response to that query, I would argue that you can supplement campuswide efforts at "honesty priming" (such as the ones that take place at orientation, or in a poster campaign) with efforts specific to your course and assignments. Course-specific priming should come first in the forms of academic honesty reminders on your syllabus. Like many instructors at my institution, I include a section of the college's academic honesty policy in my syllabus and review it with the students on the first day of the semester. While this might seem like a piece of obvious and self-evident advice, a 2008 survey of faculty at one institution found that 20 percent of them did not include a word about academic integrity on their syllabi.[1] The academic integrity statements on a syllabus can provide you with the opportunity to discuss your disciplinary reflections on original work, or aca-

demic integrity, as we discussed in a previous chapter.[2] Of course
paper or presentation assignment sheets should include basic
information about your expectations for academically honest
work. I typically will note, for example, whether I want students
to consult outside sources for their interpretation of a work of
literature, or whether I expect them to rely on our class discussions and supplemental readings. Spelling out those expectations both serves as a reminder about doing honest work and
also helps clarify for students the differences between honest and
dishonest work on any given assignment. When students are
taking major exams, you might give them an oral reminder
about doing their own work prior to the exam, and then ask
them to sign a pledge at the end of the exam stating that
they have completed the exam honestly. You can include such
pledges on any work that you assign, including papers, presentations, and homework assignments. Institutions with honor
codes frequently require that students sign such pledges in conjunction with any graded work, and again I think we can adopt
this worthwhile practice without having to adopt the larger code
itself.

In all of these efforts, keep the focus on education rather than
on the moral depravity of cheating or the dire consequences of
engaging in it (even if you spell out those consequences clearly
for them, as you probably should). Helping students understand
and adhere to the codes of academic honesty requires a continuing effort by all of us on campus, and faculty should play the
most consistent role in that educational process, with regular
reminders accompanying our assignments and exams.

Confronting Cheating

The literature here is light, and with good reason: most institutional academic integrity policies will offer guidance or even spe-

cific rules about how to confront a suspected act of cheating. Follow those guidelines. If you find them restrictive or overly bureaucratic, work to change them. I know of at least one institution that specifies that faculty members who suspect cheating should report it directly to a central office, and who thus have no ability to speak with the student about the matter until a formal hearing. Other institutions have much more open-ended policies, allowing the matter to rest entirely in the hands of the faculty member unless they choose to refer it to a central office. In this section as in the following one, I recommend strongly that you follow institutional policy, even if you don't agree with it. Patchwork responses to confronting cheaters lead both to confusion among students and to gaps that allow cheating students to slide through unpunished.

But I do have one essential piece of advice to offer in confronting cheating, even if you will find it a difficult one to follow: manage your emotions. The biggest mistake you can make in responding to a cheating incident is to take it personally. I know many faculty who see cheating as a personal affront to them, and so respond with anger, disappointment, depression, and other draining and pointless emotions. Students cheat because they are morally bankrupt or because they are responding inappropriately to a context you have structured for them. They do not cheat in order to show you up, or put one over on you, or make your life miserable. It might feel that way, but that's simply not the case. You are an obstacle in the way of their cheating, not the object of their cheating. I have seen colleagues get sucked into cases of academic dishonesty that consumed days and weeks of their lives, motivated by their desire to see the cheating student punished as severely as possible. You can imagine the toll this takes on your teaching, your research, your family life, and your health.

A student cheats on an assignment or an exam—he does not

cheat *on you*. If you have an honor code, the student has pledged his loyalty to the code, and not to you. Cheating violations are not violations against you; they are violations against the code, the policy, the course, or the assignment. You are connected to all of these things, but you are co-equal with none of them. You may have to work hard to remind yourself of this when you first suspect or confront a cheating student, because feelings of anger are perfectly understandable. Typically when I first meet with a cheating student, what I most want to say is: *Do you think I'm an idiot?* How could you possibly expect that I would not catch this? But of course the student wasn't thinking about me at all when she cheated; I was the last thing on her mind. So don't blame yourself for having emotions in response to a cheating student, but don't let them determine your response. We tend to think a lot less clearly when we are angry, and you will reduce the chances of helping the student learn from the experience if you approach the confrontation from a place of anger.

Responding to Cheating

The chances are extremely high that your institution has a clearly defined policy on how to punish cheating, whether it takes the form of the policy described in the last chapter or another form. The sanctions may come from a central office or an academic integrity board, or you may have the freedom to impose whatever sanctions you see as fitting. In either case, the chances are also extremely high that you are supposed to report incidents of cheating to a central office of some kind, either a dedicated academic integrity office or some other administrative office. But whatever the institutional policy might mandate, a faculty member can always strike a private deal with a cheating student, in which she and the cheater agree to a specific punishment—such as failing or redoing the assignment in question—in exchange for which the faculty member does not report the infraction to whatever governing body exists on her campus for academic honesty issues. Private deals like this happen for two very understandable reasons. First, many institutions make it a difficult and time-consuming process for faculty to report violations of academic honesty. The time spent tracking down the original source of a plagiarized paper and the emotional energy expended confronting the student about the matter are only the beginning; if the student appeals the decision or the penalty, faculty members can become embroiled in a long, tangled process. The reluctance of faculty to be drawn into such a time sink is intensified by the fact that cheating violations often happen during the crunch times of the semester, when you are already overburdened with papers or exams to grade. A second reason that many faculty members adduce for not reporting violations is that they feel the institution's punishments are too harsh, and that a student who copied from a peer on a homework assignment does not deserve to fail the course entirely. Therefore the faculty member may impose a lighter sentence, avoiding the one-size-fits-all punishment of the institution.

While those reasons are understandable ones, striking private deals with students is a terrible idea. The first reason we should not strike private deals with students can be deduced from some simple logical thinking about the matter. Suppose you strike a private deal with a first-semester freshman in your class, and—in your compassion and wisdom—decide to allow him to redo the assignment without penalty, in exchange for which he has to receive a lecture from you on the importance of academic honesty and promise never to do it again. Now imagine that he has classes with four other faculty members who draw from the same wells of compassion and wisdom that you do, and in whose classes he has also cheated and been allowed to redo his assignments without penalty and without any member of the administration knowing about it. Potentially this clever student could be a first-time offender in forty classes over the course of his four years of college and never once suffer any serious repercussions for his behavior. Private deals allow for the possibility of repeat offenders slipping through the cracks of the academic honesty policies on your campus, and should therefore never be made with students who have cheated in your course.

I can offer you one additional reason to avoid simply giving an offender a private slap on the wrist. Dan Ariely and his colleagues did a series of experiments that demonstrate what they call the "What the Hell" effect, by which they mean that once you commit your first act of dishonesty, you are more likely to say "Oh, what the hell" and commit more such acts of dishonesty. In one experiment, for example, in which people had multiple opportunities to cheat over the course of an extended time period, they found that "for many people there was a very sharp transition where at some point in the experiment, they suddenly graduated from engaging in a little bit of cheating to cheating at every single opportunity they had."[3] Once you begin to think of yourself as a cheater, Ariely and his colleagues theorize, and accept that self-definition, you are much more willing to engage in cheating behaviors. For this reason, Ariely writes, "we should not view a single act of dishonesty as just one petty act. We tend to forgive people for their first offense with the idea that it is just the first time and everyone makes mistakes. And although this may be true, we should also realize that the first act of dishonesty might be particularly important in shaping the way a person looks at himself and his actions from that point on."[4] According to Ariely's theory, then, our response to the first act of dishonesty that we catch is a crucial one. If we are able to convey to the student the seriousness of what he has done, we can put a roadblock in the way of the student's gradual slide into a person who is willing to engage in cheating acts at "every single opportunity" he has.

The end result of this advice is simply that, in terms of individual faculty responses to cheating, you should first and foremost follow your institutional policy on reporting cheating students to a central office or officer who can maintain records and prevent students from becoming serial offenders. If you do have the opportunity to determine a specific punishment for the student within such a policy, I would recommend that contrite students be required to redo the assignment or exam with whatever late penalties you would give them for turning in an assignment after the due date, even if that means no credit at all, if that is your policy on late work. That seems like the most sensible means you can use to determine a penalty beyond the assignment, since of course their revised and honestly completed version will indeed be coming in after the due date. If your institution does not require students to complete any kind of educational training or assignment on academic integrity, consider adding that element to your response. But don't simply load on tons of extra work or fail first-time offenders. Save such punitive measures for repeat offenders, and for the academic honesty board, and give first-time violators the merciful response we all would like to receive in response to the dumb mistakes we make in our lives.

CONCLUSION

The Future of Cheating

You will have noticed that although we have reached the conclusion, I have hardly touched on the subject of cheating and technology, or of cheating in online courses or blended courses or any other course that relies on the Web for its structure or content. You may be as surprised as I was to learn that the current research on this subject suggests that neither the rates of cheating nor the principles for addressing it are much different in virtual environments than they are in real ones. This may come as a surprise to you, especially if the grumpy professor who complains about the declining moral values of the kids these days has also informed you that students are cheating in droves in online courses.[1] You need to quit listening to that guy. In fact the small number of studies that have been done on cheating in online courses versus cheating in traditional courses suggest that the numbers are just about the same. A quick internet search on the subject will provide you with plenty of evidence, from both popular and academic sources, to demonstrate that while online courses provide students with more opportunities to cheat, those students don't seem to be doing so any more than their traditional classroom counterparts.[2] One reason for this may be, as a researcher speculated in the *Chronicle of Higher Education,* that older students are less likely to cheat than younger students, and many participants in online courses are older, nontraditional students.[3] That may change as online instruction becomes increasingly popular even at traditional universities, but for now we do not have good evidence to suggest that cheating is rampant in online courses—even though it is happening, and happening more than we would like, just like cheating in all of our courses.

The future of cheating also includes the future of technologies to prevent and reduce cheating, which are constantly evolving in response to new cheating techniques, pushing and pulling at one another uncertainly in an awkward waltz. Many institutions and faculty members now rely on plagiarism detection software, which itself of course constantly evolves in the wake of new technological developments. Smart theorists of these programs, like Sharon Flynn, the Assistant Director of the Centre for Excellence in Learning and Teaching at the National University of Ireland-Galway, will tell you that, contrary to popular belief, they do not catch plagiarists. As Flynn puts it in an excellent blog post introducing new users to the software program Turnitin.com, "Turnitin does not detect plagiarism, it highlights matching text. It is very good at what it does, but it cannot tell you that a student has plagiarised. You, as the teacher, are the one who decides if the matching text indicates a problem, or otherwise." As she also point out, the program can only detect "matching text," and will not help you with "plagiarism of ideas" or "ghost-written materials."[4] Faculty members cannot expect that running every student's paper through Turnitin or any compatible program will solve their cheating problems for them—especially since Turnitin offers a comparable service for students that allows them to submit their papers to the same database used by faculty members in order to see what their reports will look like—and, presumably, modify plagiarized text just enough to avoid detection.

Instead, faculty members who choose to make use of Turnitin and its equivalents should think of it like they think of anything else they might make use of in their teaching: as a tool that can help or hinder student learning. For example, faculty members who want to help students understand more clearly how to incorporate the words of others into their research or scholarly writing can use Turnitin's originality reports for that purpose. Projecting for students in class an originality report from an unpublished piece of academic writing—such as a forthcoming bit of your own work—will allow them to see the extent to which scholarship relies on direct quotations from the work of scholars in dialogue with the writer's original interpretations; doing so with multiple pieces of writing, and discussing it with them, will allow them to gain a general sense of the amount of original writing typically required from an academic essay in your discipline. As long as you inform students in advance that you will be doing so, projecting in class selected originality reports from your students can help accomplish the same objective, especially if the students have already seen comparable reports from published work, and can begin to make those comparisons themselves.[5]

But again, I want to back away from the specifics of this technological tool just as I want to remain distant from any of them, since it will have likely evolved and transformed into some new form by the time you are reading these words. The principles we have considered in this book for constructing an effective learning environment should help reduce cheating in both traditional and online formats, and should guide your thinking in the use of any technological tools that you avoid or deploy in the process. To give just one quick example, cheating comes easily enough in the college classroom with the use of personal response systems, or clickers. As documented in a report on the subject in the *Chronicle of Higher Education*, students have devised a variety of ways to use clickers in collaboration with their peers to cheat on in-class assignments or quizzes. The solution to this problem, posed by Derek Bruff, the author of a book on the use of click-ers in the classroom, aligns precisely with the arguments I have made in this book: "keep the clicker stakes low and accountabil-ity for cheating high."[6] The future of cheating may look differ-ent in terms of the specific forms it takes, but I am firmly con-vinced that cheating in the future—like cheating in the past and cheating in the present—will happen for understandable rea-sons, in response to a specific environment, and can best be addressed through thinking hard about that environment and making modifications that will better motivate students to learn and give them the tools they need to do so.

In that sense, I want to finish this book on a hopeful note. Higher education faculty are working today in the midst of an explosion of information on how human beings learn. From qualitative investigations like Ken Bain's *What the Best College Teachers Do* to social science research like the kind you will find in Susan Ambrose and her colleague's book *How Learning Works* or neuroscience-based presentations like James Zull's *Art of Changing the Brain,* we have available to us now more infor-mation than ever before about the physical brain, about the workings of cognition and memory, and about the implications of it all for teaching and learning. The more attention we pay to that research, and the more we think about how we can translate the findings of these researchers into our classroom practice, the less we will have to worry about cheating. Although we may al-ways be saddled with bad eggs and apples, with criminals and cheaters, with fudging and failing, we can help the majority of our students stay academically honest by doing exactly what our profession demands: becoming as informed as we possibly can about how learning works, constructing learning environments based on what that research tells us, and caring deeply that those environments are creating deep and long-term learning in our students.

NOTES

ACKNOWLEDGMENTS

INDEX

NOTES

INTRODUCTION

1. Jeffrey R. Young, "High-Tech Cheating Abounds, and Professors Bear Some Blame," *The Chronicle of Higher Education*, March 28, 2010.

I. BUILDING A THEORY OF CHEATING

1. Tricia Bertram Gallant, *Academic Integrity in the Twenty-First Century* (San Francisco: Jossey-Bass, 2008), 17–18. See pp. 13–31 for her complete history.

1. WHO CHEATS—AND HOW MUCH?

1. William J. Bowers, *Student Dishonesty and Its Control in College* (New York: Columbia University, Bureau of Applied Social Research, 1964), 7.

2. Ibid., 47.

3. Ibid.

4. "ICAI History," http://www.academicintegrity.org/icai/about-3.php (accessed August 24, 2012).

5. Donald L. McCabe and Linda Klebe Trevino, "Individual and Contextual Influences on Academic Dishonesty: A Multi-Campus Investigation," *Research in Higher Education* 38.3 (1997): 385–386.

6. Donald L. McCabe and Linda Klebe Trevino, "What We Know About Cheating in College: Longitudinal Trends and Recent Developments," *Change* 28.1 (1996): 31.

7. Donald L. McCabe, Linda Klebe Trevino, and Kenneth D. But-

terfield, "Cheating in Academic Institutions: A Decade of Research," *Ethics and Behavior* 11.3 (2001): 223.

8. Donald L. McCabe, Kenneth D. Butterfield, and Linda K. Trevino, *Cheating in College: Why Students Do It and What Educators Can Do About It* (Baltimore: Johns Hopkins University Press, 2012), loc 955 of 4211.

9. McCabe, Butterfield, and Trevino, *Cheating in College*, loc 955 of 4211.

10. Stephen F. Davis, Patrick F. Drinan, and Tricia Bertram Gallant, *Cheating in School: What We Know and What We Can Do* (West Sussex: Wiley-Blackwell, 2009).

11. McCabe, Butterfield, and Trevino, *Cheating in College*, loc 1156 of 4211.

12. Susan D. Blum, *My Word! Plagiarism and College Culture* (Ithaca: Cornell University Press, 2009), 57–58.

13. See Robert T. Burrus, KimMarie McGoldrick, and Peter W. Schuhmann, "Self-Reports of Student Cheating: Does a Definition of Cheating Matter?" *Research in Economic Education* 38.1 (Winter 2007): 3–16.

14. See Davis, Drinan, and Gallant, *Cheating in School*, 47–53, for a good discussion of shifts in student definitions and attitudes toward cheating.

15. McCabe, Butterfield, and Trevino, *Cheating in College*, loc 1149 of 4211.

16. Ibid., loc 710 of 4211.

17. See Bernard E. Whitley, Jr. and Patricia Keith-Spiegel, *Academic Dishonesty: An Educator's Guide* (New York: Psychology Press, 2001) 7.

18. Bertram Gallant, *Academic Integrity*, 29.

2. Case Studies in (the History of) Cheating

1. Nigel Spivey, *The Ancient Olympics* (Oxford: Oxford University Press, 2004), xx–xxi.

2. Ibid., 77.

3. Ibid., 165.

4. Blum, *My Word!*, 22.

5. Ichisada Miyazaki, *China's Examination Hell: The Civil Service Exams of Imperial China* (New Haven, CT: Yale University Press, 1981).

6. Conrad Schirokauer, "Introduction," in Miyazaki, *China's Examination Hell*, 7.

7. For an excellent overview of the literature of failed exam takers, see Hoi K. Suen and Lan Yu, "Chronic Consequences of High-Stakes Testing? Lessons from the Chinese Civil Service Exam," *Comparative Education Review* 50.1 (February 2006): 58–59.

8. Miyazaki, *China's Examination Hell*, 17.

9. "Ancient Chinese 'Cheat Sheets' Discovered," *The Telegraph*, July 15, 2009. http://www.telegraph.co.uk/news/worldnews/asia/china/5834418/Ancient-Chinese-cheat-sheets-discovered.html.

10. Schirokauer, "Introduction," in Miyazaki, *China's Examination Hell*, 7.

11. For a parallel case of widespread cheating within a similar context, see Daniel Del Castillo, "Cheating Widespread on Afghanistan Exams," *The Chronicle of Higher Education*, February 13, 2004. The article explains that some 6,000 exams out of 30,000 were being investigated for cheating, and notes that these exams were "the sole determinant in admissions [to Afghani universities], which puts enormous pressure on prospective university students."

12. A full copy of the No Child Left Behind Act of 2001 (PL 107-110) can be downloaded from the U.S. Department of Education website at this address: http://www2.ed.gov/policy/elsec/leg/esea02/index.html (accessed August 23, 2012).

13. Ibid., 15.

14. Ibid., 61.

15. "Educators Implicated in Atlanta Cheating Scandal," *US News and World Report*, July 7, 2011. http://www.usnews.com/education/blogs/high-school-notes/2011/07/07/educators-implicated-in-atlanta-cheating-scandal (accessed August 23, 2012).

16. For an excellent overview of the Atlanta cheating scandal and its

origins in high-stakes testing, see Dana Goldstein, "How High-Stakes Testing Led to the Atlanta Cheating Scandal," *Slate,* July 21, 2011. http://www.slate.com/articles/double_x/doublex/2011/07/how_highstakes_testing_led_to_the_atlanta_cheating_scandal.html (accessed August 23, 2012).

17. "Teachers Give No Child Left Behind Act Mixed Reviews," University of California, Riverside Newsroom, January 26, 2010. http://newsroom.ucr.edu/2245 (accessed August 23, 2012).

18. Jared Piazza, Jesse M. Bering, and Gordon Ingram, "'Princess Alice is Watching You': Children's Belief in an Invisible Person Inhibits Cheating," *Journal of Experimental Child Psychology* 109.3 (July 2011): 311. Jesse Bering confirmed for me in an email the time frame in which the experiments were conducted.

3. "Fudging" Learning Environments

1. Dan Ariely, *The (Honest) Truth about Dishonesty: How We Lie to Everyone—Especially Ourselves* (New York: HarperCollins, 2012). The "fudge factor" is first introduced and explained on pp. 26–29.

2. Ibid., 8.

3. For an excellent overview of the literature on extrinsic and intrinsic motivation, see Ken Bain, *What the Best College Teachers Do* (Cambridge, MA: Harvard University Press, 2004), 32–42. For a more thorough exploration of motivation and learning, which pushes beyond the intrinsic-extrinsic framework, see Susan A. Ambrose, Michael W. Bridges, Marsha C. Lovett, Michele DiPietro, and Marie K. Norman, *How Learning Works: 7 Research-Based Principles for Smart Teaching* (San Francisco: Jossey-Bass, 2010): 66–90.

4. Tamera B. Murdock and Eric M. Anderman, "Motivational Perspectives on Student Cheating: Toward an Integrated Model of Academic Dishonesty," *Educational Psychologist* 41.3 (2006): 131.

5. Ibid., 132.

6. Eric M. Anderman, Tripp Griesinger, and Gloria Westerfield, "Motivation and Cheating During Adolescence," *Journal of Educational Psychology* 90.1 (1998): 89.

7. Tamera B. Murdock, Angela Miller, and Julie Kohlhardt, "Effects of Classroom Context Variables on High School Students' Judgments of the Acceptability and Likelihood of Cheating," *Journal of Educational Psychology* 96.4 (2004): 771.

8. Suen and Yu, "Chronic Consequences," 60, 61.

9. George M. Diekhoff, Emily E. LaBeff, Kohei Shinohara, and Hajime Yasukawa, "College Cheating in Japan and the United States," *Research in Higher Education* 40.3 (1999): 344.

10. Ibid.

11. Ibid., 351.

12. Bowers, *Student Dishonesty,* 89–90.

13. For a more recent study that draws a link between extrinsic motivation and increased cheating behaviors, see David A. Rettinger and Yair Kramer, "Situational and Personal Causes of Student Cheating," *Research in Higher Education* 50 (2009): 293–313. They also note the positive correlation, described at the end of this chapter, between the perception of peer cheating behavior and one's own inclination to cheat.

14. Murdock and Anderman, "Motivational Perspectives," 134.

15. Ibid., 135.

16. Don McCabe and Daniel Katz, "Curbing Cheating," *NJEA Review,* September 2009: 17. See also Jason Stephens, "Justice or Just Us? What To Do About Cheating," *Carnegie Perspectives: A Different Way to Think About Teaching and Learning* http://www.carnegiefoundation.org/perspectives/, and Whitley and Keith-Spiegel, *Academic Dishonesty,* who explain that "College students' stated reasons for academic dishonesty often reflect the view that dishonesty is a legitimate response to what they perceive to be unfair treatment by an instructor, and students report cheating more often in classes conducted by instructors whom they believe treat them unfairly" (45).

17. Murdock and Anderman, "Motivational Perspectives," 135.

18. Bowers, *Student Dishonesty,* 146.

19. Ibid., 147.

20. McCabe and Trevino, "Individual and Contextual Influences," 391.

21. Ibid.

22. For a more detailed analysis of cheating among fraternity and sorority members, see Donald L. McCabe and William J. Bowers, "The Relationship between Student Cheating and College Fraternity or Sorority Membership," *NASPA Journal* 33.4 (Summer 1996): 280–291.

23. Donald L. McCabe and Linda Klebe Trevino, "Academic Dishonesty: Honor Codes and Other Contextual Influences," *Journal of Higher Education* 64.5 (1993): 533.

24. Donald L. McCabe, T. Feghali, and H. Abdallah, "Academic Dishonesty in the Middle East: Individual and Contextual Factors," *Research in Higher Education* 49.5 (2008): 463.

25. Ibid.

26. Ibid.

4. Fostering Intrinsic Motivation

1. Susan Ambrose, Michael W. Bridges, Marsha C. Lovett, Michele DiPietro, and Marie K. Norman, *How Learning Works: 7 Research-Based Principles for Smart Teaching* (San Francisco: Jossey Bass, 2010).

2. Ken Bain, *What the Best College Teachers Do* (Cambridge, MA: Harvard University Press, 2004).

3. See http://www.bestteachersinstitute.org/ for more information on Bain's summer program.

4. Ken Bain, *What the Best College Students Do* (Cambridge, MA: Harvard University Press, 2012).

5. Bain, *College Teachers,* 31.

6. Ibid., 37.

7. Ibid., 38.

8. Ibid., 39.

9. Some of the material in this chapter first appeared in James M. Lang, "The Grounded Curriculum, Part 2," *The Chronicle of Higher Education,* August 15, 2012. http://chronicle.com/article/The-Grounded-Curriculum-Part/133663/ (accessed August 24, 2012). Any information or quotations from Kaufman not directly cited are from an email interview conducted with him on July 2, 2012. All com-

ments from Kaufman's students not attributed to a publication come from unpublished documents he prepared for Bain's Summer Institute or from compilations of student responses to the course, both on video and on paper, that he provided to me.

10. "Behind Bars," With Good Reason, Virginia Foundation for the Humanities, April 30, 2011. http://withgoodreasonradio.org/2011/04/behind-bars/ (accessed August 24, 2012).

11. Andrew D. Kaufman and Hannah Ehrlinspiel, "Humans and the Humanities," *insidehighered.com,* March 14, 2011. http://www.insidehighered.com/views/2011/03/14/essay_on_what_college_students_learned_from_teaching_students_in_a_juvenile_correctional_facility (accessed August 24, 2012).

12. Ibid.

13. I first introduced the idea of "grounded" assessments in James M. Lang, "The Grounded Curriculum," *The Chronicle of Higher Education,* July 3, 2012. http://chronicle.com/article/The-Grounded-Curriculum/132679 (accessed August 24, 2012).

14. All material from Sarah Cavanagh comes from an email interview conducted on April 9, 2012.

15. Daniel Schacter, *The Seven Sins of Memory (How the Mind Forgets and Remembers)* (New York: Houghton Mifflin, 2002), 150.

16. According to another set of researchers, we are most likely to remember information that has relevance for our personal survival. They tested this with a series of experiments in which subjects had to process information in a simulated hunter-gatherer environment versus a modern city, and found that subjects had stronger memories of information processed in the hunter-gatherer environment. Unfortunately, it's difficult to see the practical implications for this particular conclusion for higher education faculty! See James S. Nairne and Josefa N. S. Pandeirada, "Adaptive Memory: Ancestral Priorities and Mnemonic Value of Survival Processing," *Cognitive Psychology* 61 (2010): 1–22.

17. For some interesting other possible ways to personalize assignments, see Lajuan Davis, "Arresting Student Plagiarism: Are We Investigators or Educators?" *Business Communication Quarterly* 74.2 (June 2011): 160–163.

5. Learning for Mastery

1. Suzanne Collins, *The Hunger Games* (New York: Scholastic, 2008).

2. "'Supersizing' the College Classroom: How One Instructor Teaches 2,670 Students," *The Chronicle of Higher Education*, April 29, 2012. http://chronicle.com/article/How-One-Instructor-Teaches/131656/ (accessed August 24, 2012).

3. Ibid.

4. Boyer's syllabus can be downloaded from his website: http://www.thejohnboyer.com/world-regions/ (accessed August 24, 2012). All material from his syllabus comes from his Spring 2011 version.

5. Any quotes from Boyer not attributed to his website come from a video in which he responded to interview questions I had sent him, and which he sent to me on June 12, 2012.

6. "New Educational Approaches," http://www.thejohnboyer.com/new-education/ (accessed August 24, 2012).

7. Ambrose et al., *How Learning Works*, 89.

8. Mark R. Young, "The Motivational Effects of the Classroom Environment in Facilitating Self-Regulated Learning," *Journal of Marketing Education* 27 (2005): 36.

9. Carole Ames, "Classrooms: Goals, Structures, and Student Motivation," *Journal of Educational Psychology* 84.3 (1992): 263.

10. Ibid., 264.

11. Ibid., 266.

12. Whitley and Keith-Spiegel, *Academic Dishonesty*, 65.

13. Ibid., 67.

6. Lowering Stakes

1. Michelle Miller, "What College Teachers Should Know About Memory: A Perspective from Cognitive Psychology," *College Teaching* 59 (2011): 117–122.

2. James M. Lang, "Teaching and Human Memory, Part 1," *The Chronicle of Higher Education*, November 15, 2011. http://chronicle.

com/article/TeachingHuman-Memory/129778/ (accessed August 25, 2012); James M. Lang, "Teaching and Human Memory, Part 2," *The Chronicle of Higher Education,* December 14, 2011. http://chronicle.com/article/TeachingHuman-Memory/130078/ (accessed August 25, 2012). Some of the material from this chapter first appeared in these two columns.

3. Jeffrey K. Karpicke and Henry L. Roediger, "The Critical Importance of Retrieval for Learning," *Science* 319 (February 15, 2008): 966.

4. Ibid., 967.

5. Ibid.

6. Mark A. McDaniel, Henry L. Roediger III, and Kathleen B. McDermott, "Generalizing Test-Enhanced Learning from the Laboratory to the Classroom," *Psychonomic Bulletin and Review* 14.2 (2007): 200–206.

7. Ibid., 203.

8. Ibid., 204.

9. Ibid., 205.

10. Miller, "College Teachers," 117.

11. Ibid., 118.

12. Ibid., 119.

13. Cathy N. Davidson, *Now You See It: How the Brain Science of Attention Will Change the Way We Live, Work, and Learn* (New York: Viking, 2011): 45.

14. For another simplified overview of some of these basic principles aimed at the general reader, see Annie Murphy Paul, "The Trouble with Homework," *New York Times,* September 10, 2011. http://www.nytimes.com/2011/09/11/opinion/sunday/quality-homework-a-smart-idea.html?pagewanted=all (accessed November 23, 2012).

15. Any quotations or material from Michelle Miller not attributed to a published source comes from email interviews conducted with her during the summer of 2012.

16. "Online Classes See Cheating Go High-Tech," *The Chronicle of Higher Education,* June 3, 2012. http://chronicle.com/article/Cheating-Goes-High-Tech/132093/ (accessed August 25, 2012).

17. Ambrose et al., *How Learning Works,* 108.

18. For my own analysis of the challenges of knowledge transfer, see my three-part series on the subject, beginning with James M. Lang, "Why They Don't Apply What They've Learned, Part I," *The Chronicle of Higher Education,* January 21, 2013, at http://chronicle.com/ article/Why-Dont-They-Apply-What/136753/ (accessed March 19, 2013). See also Lang, "Why They Don't Apply What They've Learned, Part 2," *The Chronicle of Higher Education,* February 19, 2013, at http://chronicle.com/article/Why-They-Dont-Apply-What/ 137389/ (accessed March 21, 2013); and Lang, "Why They Don't Apply What They've Learned, Part 3," *The Chronicle of Higher Education,* March 20, 2013, at http://chronicle.com/article/ Why-They-Dont-Apply-What-They/137963/ (accessed March 21, 2013).

7. Instilling Self-Efficacy

1. James M. Lang, "Metacognition and Student Learning," *The Chronicle of Higher Education,* January 17, 2012. http://chronicle. com/article/MetacognitionStudent/130327/ (accessed August 25, 2012). For Stephen Chew's video series, see "How to Get the Most Out of Studying," http://www.samford.edu/how-to-study/ (accessed August 25, 2012).

2. Quoted in Lang, "Metacognition."

3. Ibid.

4. Ibid.

5. Ibid.

6. Quotes from Stephen Chew not attributed to a source come from email interviews conducted with him during December 2011 and the summer of 2012.

7. In fact, one set of researchers demonstrated that when students received positive feedback on a test response in which they had a low sense of self-confidence, their recall of that information improved significantly. See Andrew C. Butler, Jeffrey D. Karpicke, and Henry L. Roediger III, "Correcting a Metacognitive Error: Feedback Increases

Retention of Low-Confidence Correct Responses," *Journal of Experimental Psychology* 34.4 (2008): 918–928.

8. David J. Palazzo, Young-Jin Lee, Rasil Warnakulasooriya, and David E. Pritchard, "Patterns, Correlates, and Reduction of Homework Copying," *Physics Review Special Topics–Physics Education Research* 6 (2010): 1–11.

9. Palazzo et al., "Patterns," 3–4.

10. Ibid., 4.

11. Ibid., 5.

12. Ibid., 9.

13. Ibid.

14. For an excellent description of the process of flipping a classroom, and the principles that contribute to the success of such a course redesign, see Monica Brown, Shahla Peterman, and Teresa Thiel, "Addressing the Crisis in College Mathematics: Designing Courses for Student Success," *Change* 40.4 (July–August 2008): 44–49.

15. See Derek Bruff, "Flipping Out," http://derekbruff.org/?p=2108 (accessed August 25, 2012). Bruff's blog post provides another good overview of the notion of "flipping" the classroom, with plenty of links to other resources.

16. Ambrose et al., *How Learning Works*, 134.

17. Ibid., 76.

18. Ibid., 77.

19. Ibid.

20. Ibid., 86–87.

21. James M. Lang, "Finding a Light," *The Chronicle of Higher Education*, September 17, 2012. http://chronicle.com/article/Finding-a-Light/46637/ (accessed August 25, 2012). Some of the introduction to this chapter originally appeared in that essay. All quotes from Joe Hoyle not directly attributed to a source come from email interviews conducted with him, or from materials he sent to me, in the summer of 2012.

22. Some research has suggested that strong interpersonal relationships between instructor and student, centered on a shared desire for learning, can boost student success. Hoyle's communications with his

students, both in and out of class, strike me as an ideal means of building such relationships. See Marina Micari and Pilar Pazos, "Connecting to the Professor: Impact of the Student-Faculty Relationship in a Highly Challenging Course," *College Teaching* 60.2 (2012): 41–47.

23. Joe Ben Hoyle, *Tips and Thoughts on Improving the Teaching Process—A Personal Diary*, unpublished ms. The book can be downloaded or read online for free at https://facultystaff.richmond.edu/~jhoyle/ (accessed August 25, 2012).

24. Joe Ben Hoyle, "In the Classroom, Easy Doesn't Do It," *University of Richmond Alumni Magazine* (Fall 2005): 48. http://magazine.richmond.edu/fall2005/vantage_point/index.html (accessed August 25, 2012).

25. Ibid.

26. Ambrose et al., *How Learning Works*, 88.

III. Speaking about Cheating

1. Bradley Zakarin of Northwestern University has compiled a handy list of these at http://bzeducon.com/resources.html. My thanks to him for bringing them to my attention.

2. Not to mention over time. As Tricia Bertram Gallant points out in *Academic Integrity in the Twenty-First Century*, academic misconduct in some of the early, southern honor code environments included any actions "contrary to good manners" (15).

3. Ibid., 76.

4. Whitley and Keith-Spiegel, in *Academic Dishonesty*, liken it to the infamous definition of pornography: "Academic dishonesty appears to be one of those phenomena that few people can define exactly, but that everyone can recognize when they see it," 16.

8. Cheating on Campus

1. Timothy M. Dodd, "Honor Codes 101," International Center for Academic Integrity. http://www.academicintegrity.org/icai/assets/honor_codes_101.pdf (accessed August 26, 2012).

2. Donald L. McCabe and Patrick Drinan, "Toward a Culture of Academic Integrity," *The Chronicle of Higher Education,* October 15, 1999. http://chronicle.com/article/Toward-a-Culture-of-Academic/15639 (accessed August 26, 2012).

3. Donald L. McCabe, Linda Klebe Trevino, and Kenneth D. Butterfield, "Academic Integrity in Honor Code and Non-honor Code Environments: A Qualitative Investigation," *Journal of Higher Education* 70.2 (1999): 223.

4. Ibid., 228.

5. Davis, Drinan, and Bertram Gallant, *Cheating in School,* 141.

6. Donald L. McCabe and Linda Klebe Trevino, "Academic Dishonesty: Honor Codes and Other Contextual Influences," *Journal of Higher Education* 64.5 (1993): 534.

7. Michael A. Vandehey, George M. Diekhoff, and Emily E. LaBeff, "College Cheating: A Twenty-Year Follow-Up and the Addition of an Honor Code," *Journal of College Student Development* 48.4 (2007): 476.

8. McCabe and Trevino, "Academic Dishonesty," 533.

9. McCabe and Drinan, "Culture."

10. Donald L. McCabe and Gary Pavela, "New Honor Codes for a New Generation," *insidehighered.com,* March 11, 2005. http://www.insidehighered.com/views/2005/03/11/pavela1 (accessed August 26, 2012).

11. McCabe et al., *Cheating in College,* loc 1807 of 4211.

12. For an excellent case study of the process of constructing an honor code from scratch and the full nature of the work required, see Judith Winters Spain and Marcel Marie Robes, "Academic Integrity Policy: The Journey," *Business Communication Quarterly* 74.2 (June 2011): 151–159.

13. Ambrose et al., *How Learning Works,* 108.

14. Ibid., 111.

15. Ariely, *Dishonesty,* 39.

16. Ibid., 40.

17. Ibid., 41–44.

18. Davis, Drinan, and Bertram Gallant, *Cheating in School,* 198.

19. Suzanne S. Hudd, Caroline Apgar, Eric Franklyn Bronson, Renee Gravois Lee, "Creating a Campus Culture of Integrity: Comparing the Perspectives of Full- and Part-Time Faculty," *The Journal of Higher Education* 80.2 (March/April 2009): 162.

20. Ibid., 165.

21. Davis, Drinan, and Bertram Gallant, *Cheating in School,* 168.

22. "How to Recognize Plagiarism," Indiana University Bloomington School of Education, https://www.indiana.edu/~istd/ (accessed August 26, 2012).

23. Bertram Gallant, *Academic Integrity,* 107.

24. See http://www.uwindsor.ca/aio/academic-integrity-poster-campaign (accessed November 23, 2012).

25. Donald M. McCabe, Janet M. Dukerich, and Jane E. Dutton, "The Effects of Professional Education on Values and the Resolution of Ethical Dilemmas: Business School vs. Law School Students," *Journal of Business Ethics* 13.9 (1994): 694.

26. Ibid., 695.

27. One of the most widely read recent articles on cheating in higher education was the confession of a writer for a custom-essay company, who described the hundreds of pieces of writing he had been paid to complete by students for their courses. The article begins and ends with the story of a student who needs an MBA thesis on business ethics, which he produces for her in its entirety. See Ed Dante, "The Shadow Scholar," *The Chronicle of Higher Education,* November 12, 2010.

28. Blum, *My Word!,* 57–58.

29. Bob Perry, "Exploring Academic Misconduct: Some Insights into Student Behavior," *Active Learning in Higher Education* 11.2 (2010): 105.

9. ON ORIGINAL WORK

1. For more on my Burns celebration, see James M. Lang, "Burns and Beyond," *The Chronicle of Higher Education,* May 16, 2011. You

can also watch a short video clip from the event at: http://www.youtube.com/watch?v=2jjThVdSfME.

2. Ambrose et al., *How Learning Works,* 49.

3. Bain, *Best Teachers,* 39.

10. RESPONDING TO CHEATING

1. McCabe and Trevino, "Academic Dishonesty," 391.

2. McCabe et al., "Academic Dishonesty in the Middle East," 462.

3. Vandehey et al., "College Cheating," 474.

4. Ibid., 477.

5. Don McCabe and Andrew Makowski, in a survey of such mixed composition boards, discovered that they tend to skew more heavily toward faculty and administrators. For example, only 12 percent of the surveyed boards contained enough students that a unanimous student vote could render the verdict; by contrast, 58 percent of the boards contained enough faculty or administrators that a unanimous vote on their part could render the verdict. McCabe and Makowski argue that giving students more control in the process may ultimately result in lower rates of cheating on campus. Donald L. McCabe and Andrew L. Makowski, "Resolving Allegations of Academic Dishonesty: Is There a Role for Students to Play?" *About Campus,* March–April 2001: 17–21.

6. For one interesting example of an educational assignment that faculty can provide to students on cheating, see Leda Nath and Michael Lavaglia, "Cheating on Multiple-Choice Exams: Monitoring, Assessment, and an Optional Assignment," *College Teaching* 57.1 (Winter 2009): 3–8. The authors ask the students to complete a research paper which has two components: "the students' personal and moral history leading up to and including a detailed account of the cheating incident," followed by "library research on ethical behavior" (5).

7. Bertram Gallant, *Academic Integrity,* 71.

8. Although, as McCabe and Makowski point out, faculty members have to be careful not to bully innocent students into signing a settle-

ment form just to avoid an administrative hearing. McCabe and Makowski, "Allegations," 20.

11. Cheating in Your Classroom

1. Rebecca Volpe, Laura Davidson, and Matthew C. Bell, "Faculty
Attitudes and Behaviors Concerning Student Cheating," *College Student Journal* 42.1 (March 2008): 164–175.

2. And, of course, some faculty choose to extend this discussion to
greater lengths by giving students fuller materials, or even assignments,
on academic integrity at the outset of the semester. Bill Taylor, an
emeritus political scientist, writes his students a letter about the importance of academic integrity in his course and their college career. He
makes the letter available online for others to consider and adapt—with
proper credit, naturally. You can find a PDF version here: http://www.
jmu.edu/honor/wm_library/Letter%20To%20My%20Students.htm
(accessed November 23, 2012).

3. Ariely, *Dishonesty*, 130.

4. Ibid., 137.

Conclusion

1. His perception would be a common one, though. In one study of
student perceptions of cheating in online courses, the majority of them
felt that "more cheating occurs in online courses" and that "it is easier
to cheat in an online versus a traditional course." See Chula G. King,
Roger W. Guyette, Jr., and Chris Piotrowski, "Online Exams and
Cheating: An Empirical Analysis of Business Students' Views," *The
Journal of Educators Online* 6.1 (January 2009): 7.

2. See, for example, Donald L. McCabe and Jason M. Stephens,
"'Epidemic' as Opportunity: Internet Plagiarism as a Lever for Cultural Change," *Teachers College Record,* November 30, 2006. For a
more recent analysis, George Watson and James Sottile, "Cheating
in the Digital Age: Do Students Cheat More in Online Courses?" *Online Journal of Distance Learning Administration* XIII.I (Spring

2010): 1–10. http://www.westga.edu/~distance/ojdla/spring131/ watson131.html (accessed August 26, 2012).

3. "Do Students Cheat More in Online Courses? Maybe Not," *The Chronicle of Higher Education,* September 16, 2009. http://chronicle. com/blogs/wiredcampus/do-students-cheat-more-in-online-classes-maybe-not/8073 (accessed August 26, 2012).

4. Sharon Flynn, "Getting Started with Turnitin," http://learn techgalway.blogspot.com/2012/01/getting-started-with-turnitin. html (accessed August 26, 2012).

5. The use of plagiarism detection software can also have a symbolic function, as two researchers from the Netherlands have argued. Requiring students to turn in papers through such a program "creates a routine that strongly discourages attempts to cheat and at the same time keeps reminding students of the issue at hand [i.e., academic integrity]." See Hanny den Ouden and Carel van Wijk, "Plagiarism: Punish or Prevent? Some Experiences with Academic Copycatting in the Netherlands," *Business Communication Quarterly* 74.2 (June 2011): 196–200.

6. Jie Jenny Zou, "With Cheating Only a Click Away, Professors Reduce the Incentive," *The Chronicle of Higher Education,* September 4, 2011.

ACKNOWLEDGMENTS

One of the first books on cheating I encountered in my research was Tricia Bertram Gallant's *Academic Integrity in the Twenty-First Century,* an ASHE Higher Education Report that I highly recommend to readers interested in this topic. After offering excellent overviews of the history of cheating and analyses of the different approaches that have been taken to combat it in higher education, on page 87 of her report Bertram Gallant proposes a new strategy: "The essence of this strategy is the reframing of the main practical question from 'how do we stop students from cheating?' to 'how do we ensure students are learning?'" Her brief report offers just a few pages of reflection in response to this question, but I was struck immediately at the sensible and practical nature of this approach. One way to consider the book you are holding in your hand would be as an attempt to plot out more fully Bertram Gallant's recommended strategy, and so I am grateful to her book for stimulating me to ask and attempt to answer this question.

I am also most grateful to the faculty guides for Part II, all of whom patiently and fully responded to my requests for help, and happily answered the questions I posed to them: Andrew Kaufman, Sarah Cavanagh, John Boyer, Michelle Miller, Stephen Chew, and Joe Hoyle. I consulted with two other guides who helped shape my thinking but whose work ultimately did not appear so prominently in the manuscript, and so I am grateful as well to Owen Sholes and Sharon Flynn.

Alison Marinelli served as a research assistant for a short period, and helped hunt down many of the articles cited in this book, especially the extensive body of research conducted by Donald McCabe and his colleagues.

Three reader reports on the initial manuscript offered me excellent advice in more ways than I can enumerate here, and I am grateful for their suggestions (even if I did not always feel that way at the time!).

A number of other readers were kind enough to respond to versions of the manuscript along the way and provide constructive feedback, including Bradley Zakarin, Mike Land, Rachel Ramsey, Jenny Morrison, Eloise Knowlton, and Ken Moore all the way from Jakarta. Tony Lang, as always, read and helped.

Ken Bain has been my mentor in all things teaching and learning since I began thinking about these matters in the late 1990s, and he gave me my first opportunity to present the results of my research at his Best Teachers Summer Institute in the summer of 2012. I remain immensely grateful for his ongoing guidance and support of my work.

Elizabeth Knoll and Harvard University Press have made writing books such a pleasant experience that I hope yet to write many more. The idea for this book first came about as a suggestion from Elizabeth, and we hashed out the first possibilities at a wonderful lunch in the summer of 2011. I am grateful to her for suggesting this book project to me, and for her editorial guidance along the way.

During the summer of 2012, while I was finishing the manuscript, I brought on our family vacations a large box of books and articles on cheating—affectionately referred to as the "box o' cheating"—and stole time away from my family in order to ensure that I completed the book on deadline. I apologize for those stolen moments and hope to make them up someday soon. Thanks as always to Anne, Katie, Madeleine, Jillian, Lucie, and Jack for putting up with a writing husband and father.

My model of integrity in all areas of life, for my whole life, has been my father. He taught me what it meant to live honestly, and continues to exemplify those teachings in his own life. I can trace back all of my own small accomplishments to his influence, and remain ever grateful for the blessing of such a father. Thanks, Dad.

INDEX

Index